EDUCATION Re-formed

A Guide to the Education Reform Act
Third Edition

Stuart Maclure

Hodder & Stoughton
LONDON SYDNEY AUCKLAND

ISBN 0 340 57016 4

First published 1988

Second Edition 1989
Third Edition 1992
Third impression 1992

Photoset in Linotron Times by
Rowland Phototypesetting Ltd, Bury St Edmunds, Suffolk
Printed and bound in Great Britain for
the education division of Hodder and Stoughton Ltd,
Mill Road, Dunton Green, Sevenoaks, Kent,
by Athenaeum Press Ltd, Newcastle upon Tyne

Contents

Acknowledgements

This is a book for lay people by a lay man. If you want legal advice, consult a lawyer. This is not, and does not pretend to be, a legal text. It is designed to help readers find their way round a long and complicated piece of legislation, and to have some appreciation of the background issues.

While reserving to myself responsibility for all errors and omissions, I would like to put on record the help I have received from colleagues at *The Times Educational Supplement*, notably from Patricia Rowan and from Barry Hugill and Sue Surkes who were among those who covered the Education Reform Bill in its long and arduous passage through Parliament; from Elaine Hines in the TES library, and Janette Wolf who typed the manuscript. I must thank Charles Knight and his colleagues at Hodder and Stoughton for the speed with which the publishers have moved to produce this volume; and of course, my wife whose practical help in finalising the manuscript and clearing the proofs has been invaluable.

Two chapters benefit from material prepared for other purposes. Chapters 2 and 4 draw on a lecture entitled 'Opting In and Opting Out' given at the University of London Institute of Education in February 1988. Chapter 10 draws on a paper given to the Standing Conference on Studies in Education and published in the *British Journal of Educational Studies*, volume XXXIII, No. 2, June 1985.

Introduction

The Education Reform Act of 1988 was the most important and far-reaching piece of educational law-making for England and Wales since the Education Act of 1944.

Why? Because it altered the basic power structure of the education system.

It increased the powers of the Secretary of State for Education and Science (and, where appropriate, the Secretary of State for Wales). It restored to the central government powers over the curriculum which had been surrendered between the Wars, and set up formal machinery for exercising and enforcing these powers and responsibilities.

Not only did it strengthen the central government's role in education, it introduced important limitations on the functions of the local education authorities, who were forced to give greater autonomy to schools and governing bodies.

The change in the power structure extended to higher education. Universities and polytechnics (and other colleges of higher education) were brought more firmly under the control of the Secretary of State, through changes in their funding aimed at increasing accountability and making them more amenable to government direction. Note that the sections which relate to the universities also apply to Scotland. The rest of the Act only concerns England and Wales. Scotland has its own education laws. Scottish law has now been changed to set up school boards (much like school governing bodies in England) preparatory to the application to Scottish education of all or some of the principles behind the English Act. The Act does not extend to Northern Ireland.

It is important to recognise the radical nature of the Act at the outset. In later chapters the separate major provisions will be summarised and discussed. First it is necessary to look at the wood rather than the individual trees.

The Act was intended to mark a radical shift in direction. Mr Kenneth Baker made this clear in his opening speech in the Second Reading debate in the House of Commons on 1 December 1987. The education system, he said, had operated for more than forty years on the basis of R. A. Butler's 1944 Act, which in turn built on the Balfour Act of 1902. 'We need to inject a new vitality into that system', said Mr Baker. 'It has become 'producer-dominated.'

The charge of producer-domination had been advanced, albeit in muted form, more than ten years earlier by the then Prime Minister, James Callaghan, in his seminal Ruskin College address (18 October 1976). He noted the hostility of 'some people' to the idea of a Prime Minister intervening in the educational debate: 'It is almost', he said, 'as though some people would wish that the subject matter and purpose of education should not have public attention focused on it; or at any rate, that profane hands should not be allowed to touch it.' He went on to list complaints about the standards of attainment and vocational preparation of school-leavers and to preface his call for a Great Debate with a stern warning:

> 'to the teachers I would say that you must satisfy the parents and industry that what you are doing meets their requirements and the needs of their children. For if the public is not convinced then the profession will be laying up trouble for itself in the future.'

There is a sense, therefore, in which the 1988 Act was, as Conservative ministers insisted, the belated product of Mr Callaghan's Great Debate. There was a recognisable consensus of opinion against the educational establishment. This stretched across political and social divisions to accuse the functionaries of the system of subordinating the needs of children to their own interests and convenience.

True or false, the accusation had gathered credence as a result of two developments during the years leading up to 1988. The first was the teachers' pay dispute, which caused disruption in many schools. The dispute dragged on over a period of three years or more, and only ended with a pay settlement and a new teachers' contract being imposed by the Government and enforced by the Teachers' Pay and Conditions Act 1987. In the course of the dispute the teachers' unions became highly unpopular; having taken on the Government and lost, they were in no position to resist the attack on the education professionals which the 1988 Act presaged.

Second, the steady deterioration in the relationships between central and local government had a direct bearing on education. Local politics had became fiercer and more polarised. And among the Labour-controlled councils, which formed a majority of local education authorities, a few mavericks like Liverpool, Brent and Haringey fell into the hands of the hard Left. Determined to confront the central Government at every turn, they refused to cut expenditure in line with Government demands and incurred financial penalties including rate-capping. In education, some sought to intervene (not particularly effectively) in the curriculum, in pursuit of their own active policies on race, gender and (in some cases) sexual orientation. The scale of the hard Left activities in local government during this period was always small, but it was significant because it opened up a new, uncompromising hostility between the centre and the periphery in British politics.

The so-called 'loony left' authorities had an influence out of all proportion to their numbers in crystalising the case against the 'producers' in education, for under the 1944 Education Act it was these ideologically committed, resolutely high-spending politicians who formed the local authorities responsible for the maintained schools and colleges in their areas.

The Education Reform Bill had, therefore, to be seen against the background of a deep crisis in local government. There was an obvious need to make clear, once and for all, that national political power overrides local political power – that the national franchise takes precedence over the local. For education, that meant a revision of the distribution of power laid down in the 1944 Education Act, and a clear assertion of the leading role of the Secretary of State.

We shall return to these background issues in Chapter 10. So great has been the change in the climate of opinion about education in England and Wales since the heady days after the Second World War that to put the Act fully in context requires a chapter of its own.

•   •   •

For many reasons the change in the power structure was highly controversial. It reversed a long tradition of local policy-making and administration. It gave the Department of Education a greater executive role than ever before. It broke with the conventions which had grown up in the previous forty years, summed up in the pithy, but never wholly accurate, phrase 'a national service, locally administered'.

Because the change was so controversial, and because the increase in the powers of the Secretary of State seemed to raise quasi-constitutional issues in the minds of some critics, Mr Kenneth Baker was extremely sensitive to charges that he was assuming dictatorial powers over the education service.

He pointed to the first section of the 1944 Education Act – the brave declaratory passage which lays down the duty of the minister to:

> 'promote the education of the people of England and Wales . . . and to secure the effective execution by local authorities under his control and direction of the national policy for providing a varied and comprehensive educational service in every area.'

The role given to the Secretary of State by the Education Reform Bill, Mr Baker told the North of England Education Conference on 6 January 1988, was consistent with this duty, and necessary to enable him to carry out the national policy the law required him to have.

He claimed that the Act was only incidentally about extending the powers of central government: its main aim, he insisted, was to enhance 'the life chances of young people'. To achieve this, certain ministerial powers were strengthened and, elsewhere in the Act, certain forms of devolution were imposed on local authorities. 'It is not', he insisted defiantly, 'about enhancing central control.'

Does this mean, then, that it is wrong to stress – as I do – the change in the basic power structure of the education system as the key to the significance of this Act? Not at all. The change is indisputable, and clearly the authors of the Act believed it to be essential to their purposes. It is not the *fact* of the change in the power structure which was in dispute, but the merits or demerits of the change.

•   •   •

The change in the structure went beyond a simple trade-off of more power for the Secretary of State and less for the local education authorities. The Act also increased the autonomy of the schools and colleges which constitute the education system, the assumption being that more autonomous institutions would be more efficient and achieve higher standards.

There is an apparent paradox between more power to the centre and more autonomy at the periphery, but it may not be a real one. The argument behind the 1988 Act is that it is only possible to take the risks inherent in setting schools free of the local authorities' leading reins if there is a clearly defined national curriculum in being, and if the Secretary of State has the power to prescribe and police it. Schools could only be given day-to-day control over their own affairs if there were established conventions, reinforced if need be by ministerial authority, within which their independence could be exercised.

Some agreement along these lines was necessary to hold together both the assertion of stronger central authority and the release of local initiative. The paradox remained an uneasy balance of contradictions, like the confusion which attended the professional role of teachers in the new dispensation. On the one hand, the Reform Act (and in particular, the national curriculum) completed the restriction of the teachers' professional autonomy begun by the pay settlement and contract of service imposed by the Teachers' Pay and Conditions Act 1987. On the other hand, it sought to liberate teachers (and particularly heads) from the control of local education authorities and their administrators, in the belief that more freedom would enable them to be more efficient. In other words, teachers whose professional autonomy was to be curbed by a new contract and a national curriculum, were also to be given more professional freedom because this was a *sine qua non* of high standards.

In the pages which follow there are a number of themes to which the discussion will return. One is competition between schools. Another is the role of governors and, in particular, parents in running schools. A third is the tension between 'parent power' and the providers – the local authorities and the Churches. A fourth is the impact on planning of the change in the distribution of power, and the challenge to the assumption made hitherto that schools – whether country or voluntary – were to be managed as an interdependent system, not as isolated, auto-nomous, units.

Competition as a spur to quality is a basic concern of the Education Reform Act. By ensuring under the proposals for financial delegation (see below) that school budgets would directly and quickly reflect their popularity or unpopularity, the Act aimed to give incentives to professional teachers and lay governors alike to 'sell' their schools to the best advantage. In theory, at least, this would result in more power to parents and other consumers, in a flexible and open system.

It would be too much to say that the Act created a free market in education – this particular market is heavily and inevitably constrained, and the strengthened role of the Secretary of State as monitor of the curriculum and arbiter of the efficiency of the system is recognition that, as things now stand, this must be so. But it is clearly a step in the free-market direction.

It could be observed, with justification, that the system which had been developed since 1944 had failed to produce a homo-geneous standard of service: its chief characteristic was its patchiness. It reflected an egalitarian ideology within a system of increasingly unequal performance. What the Education Reform Act of 1988 did was to dispose of the ideology of the local education authority as the principal provider, the universal agent for the achievement of equal opportunity. Instead of patchiness being one of the acknowledged defects of the system, diversity (the other side of the same coin) would henceforth become its prime virtue. Equality of opportunity had turned out to be a contradiction in terms. The 1988 Act offered an alternative ideology with the emphasis on *opportunity*, not equality, and paved the way – if future Governments should choose to go down that road – for more complete privatisation, perhaps via a voucher system.

The 1988 Act, like the 1986 Act before it, laid great responsibilities on school governors, who held a key position in all plans for the decentralisation of the administration of the education system. Governors were among the major beneficiaries of the redistribution of power. Yet nobody could predict from experience what this would mean in practice. The Act could prescribe the powers and duties of governors, but it could not guarantee who would come forward nor how wisely they would exercise those powers and duties. There seemed to be an implied assumption that if local authority politicians were forced into a minority, governing bodies would eschew party politics and treat every matter on its merits. Given the central role ascribed to these reformed governing boards, much will depend on whether, as time passes, this assumption proves correct. Given the heat which educational controversies can generate, it would be unsurprising if some governing bodies became highly politicised.

The same processes, devised to reduce the influence of the local authorities on all maintained schools, impinge directly on the Churches, the other (often forgotten) main partner in the education system. The increase in school-based decision-making has reduced the scope for system-wide planning by the Diocesan Authorities for the Voluntary Aided Schools, the great majority of which are Church of England and Roman Catholic foundations. The procedures for acquiring Grant Maintained status (see Chapter 4) have particular implications for the voluntary school governors: they could bring governors into conflict with their trustees and, in extreme circumstances, lead to schools being removed from the system of Roman Catholic or Anglican schools within an area, against the wishes of the diocesan authorities.

Till the passing of the 1988 Education Act, it was possible to speak of the schools of a local authority forming a 'system', and for them to be treated as a 'system' for planning purposes. The same could be said of the Roman Catholic schools in a diocese, their number and location being determined by the perceived obligation to provide for the collective needs of all Roman Catholic children.

The change in the distribution of a power under the 1988 Act undermined the notion of a local or diocesan 'system' of schools, and created instead a network of separate, semi-autonomous institutions maintained by local authorities or the central government. The same changes altered the planning function, substituting market concepts of demand for planners' analysis of need, and moving in the direction of a distribution of resources according to consumer choice instead of administrative discrimination.

These are some of the reasons why the Education Reform Act of 1988 justified the importance attached to it by Margaret Thatcher as one of the key measures of her third administration's legislative programme. Now it is time to look at the new law in more detail.

1

The National Curriculum and Assessment

Sections 1 to 25

1.—(1) It shall be the duty—

    (a) of the Secretary of State as respects every maintained school;

    (b) of every local education authority as respects every school maintained by them; and

    (c) of every governing body or head teacher of a maintained school as respects that school;

to exercise their functions (including, in particular, the functions conferred on them by this Chapter with respect to religious education, religious worship and the National Curriculum) with a view to securing that the curriculum for the school satisfies the requirements of this section.

The Education Reform Act requires all maintained schools to provide for all pupils, within the years of compulsory schooling, a basic curriculum 'to be known as the national curriculum'. Section 1(2) notes that the curriculum for a maintained school 'satisfies the requirements of this section if it is a balanced and broadly based curriculum which:
(a) promotes the spiritual, moral, cultural, mental and physical development of pupils at the school and of society; and
(b) prepares such pupils for the opportunities, responsibilities and experiences of adult life.'

    Section 3 designates three core subjects and seven foundation subjects which must be taught. The core subjects are mathematics, English and science. The foundation subjects are history, geography, technology, music, art, physical education and (at the secondary stage) a modern language. Welsh is a core subject for Welsh-speaking schools and a foundation subject in non-Welsh-speaking schools in Wales.

The curriculum includes religious education for all pupils (Section 2). It must specify in relation to each subject 'the knowledge, skills and understanding which all pupils of different abilities and maturities' are expected to have learned by the end of each 'key stage' – that is, by about the ages of 7, 11, 14 and 16 (the 'attainment targets'). It must also set out how pupils are to be assessed and tested at around the prescribed ages ('the assessment arrangements').

2.—(1) The curriculum for every maintained school shall comprise a basic curriculum which includes—

> (a) provision for religious education for all registered pupils at the school; and
>
> (b) a curriculum for all registered pupils at the school of compulsory school age (to be known as 'the National Curriculum') which meets the requirements of subsection (2) below.

(2) The curriculum referred to in subsection (1)(b) above shall comprise the core and other foundation subjects and specify in relation to each of them—

> (a) the knowledge, skills and understanding which pupils of different abilities and maturities are expected to have by the end of each key stage (in this Chapter referred to as 'attainment targets');
>
> (b) the matters, skills and processes which are required to be taught to pupils of different abilities and maturities during each key stage (in this Chapter referred to as 'programmes of study'); and
>
> (c) the arrangements for assessing pupils at or near the end of each key stage for the purpose of ascertaining what they have achieved in relation to the attainment targets for that stage (in this Chapter referred to as 'assessment arrangements') . . .

Note that although a list of subjects is specified in the Act, most of the implementation – such as, for example, the setting of attainment targets, the prescription of programmes of study and the outline arrangements for assessment – is by secondary legislation in the form of Orders. The original list of subjects, too, can be amended by Order.

3.—(1) Subject to subsection (4) below, the core subjects are—

    (a) mathematics, English and science; and

    (b) in relation to schools in Wales which are Welsh-speaking schools, Welsh.

(2) Subject to subsection (4) below, the other foundation subjects are—

    (a) history, geography, technology, music, art and physical education:

    (b) in relation to the third and fourth key stages, a modern foreign language specified in an order of the Secretary of State; and

    (c) in relation to schools in Wales which are not Welsh-speaking schools, Welsh...

All maintained schools are under a general duty to make sure the national curriculum is implemented (Section 10) – that is to say, a duty is placed on the local authority and school governors in respect of county and voluntary schools (other than Aided schools) and on the governors of Aided schools and Grant Maintained schools (see Chapter 4).

4.—(1) It shall be the duty of the Secretary of State...

    (a) to establish a complete National Curriculum as soon as is reasonably practicable (taking first the core subjects and then the other foundation subjects); and

    (b) to revise that Curriculum whenever he considers it necessary or expedient to do so.

(2) The Secretary of State may by order specify in relation to each of the foundation subjects—

    (a) such attainment targets;

    (b) such programmes of study; and

    (c) such assessment arrangements;

as he considers appropriate for that subject...

Religious worship and religious education are covered in Sections 6 to 13. Section 6 states the legal requirement for a single act of worship for all pupils, or separate acts of worship for pupils of different age groups or in different school groups. In county schools, responsibility for arranging the form of worship lies with the headteacher after consultation with the governors. In voluntary schools it is the other way round: the governors are meant to make the arrangements after consultation with the head.

The Act adds the rider that in county schools the collective worship 'shall be wholly or mainly of a broadly Christian character' (Section 7(1). This is qualified by giving schools some discretion to vary the form, provided that 'taking any school term as a whole' most assemblies comply. Among the considerations which may be taken into account (Section 7(5)) are the family background of the pupils. Where heads consider that insistence on a Christian act of daily worship should not apply, they can (Section 12) submit an application to the local Standing Advisory Council on Religious Education (SACRE), which body can decide whether or not the school should have exemption, having regard to the nature of the school community. (SACREs are committees set up by local authorities with representatives of the Churches to oversee the RE curriculum.)

Religious education

6.—(1) ... All pupils in attendance at a maintained school shall on each school day take part in an act of collective worship...

7.—(1) ... In the case of a county school the collective worship ... shall be wholly or mainly of a broadly Christian character...

Religious education continues to be non-denominational in character in county and Controlled schools, based on Agreed Syllabuses. These, too, are the responsibility of the SACREs, and Section 8 lays down that they 'shall reflect the fact that the religious traditions in Great Britain are in the main Christian, while taking account of the teaching and practices of the other principal religions represented in Great Britain.'

The Act goes on (Section 14) to provide for two Curriculum Councils (one for England, one for Wales) and a School Examinations and Assessment Council to advise the Secretary of State on matters relating to the curriculum and its assessment.

All the members are nominated by him. The Act specifically requires him (Section 20(2)) to refer proposed Orders relating to the subject requirements, attainment targets and programmes of study, to the National Curriculum Council, and obliges the Council to consult with local authorities, governors' representatives, teachers' organisations and others (subsection 3). The Secretary of State must publish the advice he receives from the Council, and if he fails to follow it, state his reasons (sub-section (5)(a)(ii)).

The Secretary of State has also a general power to make regulations (Section 17) removing or modifying the provisions of the national curriculum in such circumstances as may be specified.

Special cases

18. The special educational provision for any pupil specified in a statement under section 7 of the 1981 Act of his special educational needs may include provision—

    (a) excluding the application of the provisions of the National Curriculum; or

    (b) applying those provisions with such modifications as may be specified in the statement.

19.—(1) The Secretary of State may make regulations enabling the head teacher of any maintained school, . . .

    (a) to direct as respects a registered pupil . . . the provisions of the National Curriculum—
        (i) shall not apply; or
        (ii) shall apply with such modifications as may be so specified . . .

(2) The conditions prescribed by the regulations shall . . . limit the period that may be specified . . . to a maximum period specified in the regulations . . .

(3) Where a head teacher gives a direction under regulations made under this section . . . he shall give the information mentioned in subsection (4) below, . . .

    (a) to the governing body; and

    (b) where the school is a county, voluntary or maintained special school, to the local education authority;

and . . . also to a parent of the pupil.

    (4) That information is the following—

    (a) the fact that he has taken the action in question, its effect and his reasons for taking it;

    (b) the provision that is being or is to be made for the pupil's education during the operative period of the direction; and

(c) either—

(i) a description of the manner in which he proposes to secure the full implementation in relation to the pupil after the end of that period of the provisions of the National Curriculum; or

(ii) an indication of his opinion that the pupil has or probably has special educational needs by virtue of which the local education authority would be required to determine the special educational provision that should be made for him (whether initially or on a review of any statement of his special educational needs the authority are for the time being required under section 7 of the 1981 Act to maintain)....

(6) It shall be the duty of a local education authority, on receiving information given to the authority under this section by the head teacher of any maintained school which includes such an indication of opinion with respect to a pupil, to consider whether any action on their part is required in the case of that pupil under section 5 of the 1981 Act (assessment of special educational needs).

Certain exceptions to the provisions of the Act on the national curriculum are outlined in Sections 16–19. Section 16 sets out the limited conditions under which the Secretary of State may issue a direction exempting a school from the requirements laid down in the national curriculum or modifying them. Such a direction can be given in a county, Controlled or maintained special school on the application of the local authority with the agreement of the governing body, or vice versa; or of the Curriculum Council with the agreement of both the local authority and the governing body. In a Grant Maintained, Aided or Special Agreement school, applications can be made by the governing body, or by the Curriculum Council with the governors' agreement.

There is provision in Sections 18 and 19 for pupils with special educational needs who are unable to cope with the national curriculum as laid down in the various Parliamentary Orders. For pupils whose needs have been the subject of a Statement under the 1981 Act, 'provision may exclude the application of the provisions of the national curriculum', or the national curriculum may be applied with such modifications as may be specified in the Statement. Section 19 lays down a procedure for suspending or modifying the requirements of the national curriculum in respect of particular pupils (for example, those awaiting Statementing) for limited periods, under regulations made by the Secretary of State.

An added flexibility is provided in Section 19, under which the Secretary of State can make regulations enabling the headteacher of any maintained school to modify the national curriculum in respect of any pupil for a limited period.

In reporting such action to the parent, the governors and the local authority, the head can either press for a Statement of special educational need, or signify how he or she intends to secure in due course that the pupil is brought back onto the full national curriculum course. The Section provides for the parents to have right of appeal to the governors, in respect of any action by the head under these regulations.

An important aim of the introduction of a national curriculum is to give parents the maximum information about the programmes their children are following, and regular reports on their progress. Section 22 of the Act empowers the Secretary of State to make regulations about the supply of public information which local authorities, governors and heads may be required to provide. Among the topics covered would be the details of how the national curriculum is to be interpreted, and the curriculum policy documents which all authorities and governing bodies are required to produce under the 1986 Education Act.

There is also a general power for the Secretary of State to require the local education authorities, governors and heads to provide any other information about the education of pupils that he thinks fit.

The Secretary of State's power to demand information also means that he can insist on the publication of results of assessment and testing, and determine the form which this must take.

Section 23 requires local authorities to establish their own procedures (approved by the Secretary of State and therefore subject to his guidelines) for dealing with complaints about any maintained or county and voluntary or maintained special school, including complaints that the curriculum has not been followed, or that there has been a failure to provide all the information required under Section 22.

A new orthodoxy

The powers which the Secretary of State has taken to prescribe the curriculum are similar in effect to powers which existed under the Codes which governed elementary and secondary education under the 1902 Act. These powers continued till the 1944 Act, though from the mid-1920s their application was relaxed. When the 1944 Education Act was passed, legal control of the curriculum in maintained schools was ascribed to the local education authorities and the governors of Aided schools. In practice, they never exercised their powers over the curriculum, which to all intents and purposes became the responsibility of heads and their senior staff. The external examinations exerted a strong influence in the upper forms. So too, in some local authorities, did the local advisers and other support staff.

In the decade before the introduction of the Education Reform Bill, the Department of Education and Science and successive Secretaries of State showed increasing interest in the curriculum, and began to intervene by issuing a series of policy documents such as the *Organization and Content of the 5–16 Curriculum* (1984), *Science 5–16: a Statement of Policy* (1985) and *Modern Languages in the School Curriculum* (1988).

Her Majesty's Inspectors also increased their output of curriculum papers, and local education authorities were encouraged by DES circulars to review their own curriculum arrangements.

By the time Sir Keith Joseph (Secretary of State, 1981–86) issued his White Paper on *Better Schools* (1985), it had become clear that curriculum policy had to be considered at three levels: the *national* level in the form of statements of policy issued by the Secretary of State; the *local authority* level in the form of each authority's policy statement, which would be expected to have regard to national aims and priorities; and the *school* level, where each governing body would be required to produce its own curriculum paper.

The 1986 Act, mainly concerned with reforming the composition of school governing bodies and extending their powers, demonstrated the potential danger of the three-way stretch which might arise if the Secretary of State, the local authority and the school pulled in different directions. It seemed to leave the head in the invidious position of arbitrating between his or her governors and the local authority if a disagreement were to arise.

Though *Better Schools* (paragraph 37) stated that the Government had no intention to introduce legislation redefining responsibility for the curriculum, shortly after Mr Kenneth Baker had succeeded Sir Keith Joseph in the early summer of 1986 he had begun to move towards a centrally controlled curriculum.

What had still been regarded as a highly controversial idea in the early 1980s, had become commonplace by the time it figured in the Conservative election manifesto at the General Election of June 1987. It soon became apparent that it enjoyed a wide measure of political support outside the Conservative party, and controversy concentrated not on *whether* there should be a national curriculum but on the mechanics of it and the setting of attainment targets and methods of assessment.

The 1988 Act made it clear exactly where the legal control of the curriculum lay – with the Secretary of State. It removed the confusion built into the 1986 Act, while still insisting that both the local authority and the governing body must adopt curriculum policies to give effect to the national curriculum.

The local authority's curriculum role is downgraded. It is the national curriculum which provides the local authority, the governors and the headteacher with their marching orders. A school which is implementing the national curriculum is working within the law.

The distinction which the Act made in Section 3, between the core and foundation subjects, is more important as a guide to administrative action than as a fine legal distinction.

The core subjects, as their name implies, form the central part of the curriculum. It was with these subjects that the setting up of the national curriculum would begin. Working groups were set up in Mathematics and Science, followed by Technology and English. By the summer of 1989 those in Mathematics, Science and English had reported, and the Secretary of State had published these with his own proposals.

In due course Orders were made for all the core subjects in time for the introduction of the first stages of the National Curriculum in 1989 and 1990. Draft Orders for Modern Languages, Geography and History were issued in the summer of 1991 and proposals for Art, Music and Physical Education followed.

The Act is at pains to describe the process by which the Secretary of State is to arrive at his curriculum Orders, the documents which he must lay before Parliament for a positive resolution in both Houses. Any proposals have to be referred to the appropriate Curriculum Council. The Council then puts them out for consultation with local authorities, teachers' bodies, representatives of governing bodies and 'any other persons' thought to be worth consulting. The Council then reports back to the Secretary of State, summarising the views of those consulted and making its own recommendations. The Council can also add any other advice it thinks fit.

The Secretary of State is then obliged to publish the Curriculum Council's report. He does not have to accept the advice, but if he fails to do so he must state his reasons for setting it aside. He then issues his draft Order, after which there has to be yet another period of at least a month for further consultation and representations from interested groups.

The reason for laying down such a detailed procedure was to make sure that the strong central powers vested in the Secretary of State are constrained by a due process which ensures extensive consultation and requires the Secretary of State to act publicly and explain himself.

The statutory duties of the Secondary Schools Examinations and Assessment Council and (particularly) the National Curriculum Council, more or less guaranteed that their relationship with the Secretary of State would be strenuous. Ministers have not hesitated to tell both Councils what advice they wanted; and to put it about that the Councils were unregenerate organs of the Educational Establishment when they have failed to come to heel.

Relations deteriorated during the second half of 1990 and the first half of 1991. In the summer of 1991, the chairmen of both councils were sacked. To replace them, the then Secretary of State, Mr Kenneth Clarke, appointed Lord Griffiths, an ex-head of the Downing Street Policy Unit (as chairman of SEAC) and another ex-member of the Unit, Mr David Paschal (as chairman of NCC). One of the matters at issue was how to deal with Key Stage 4 (see page 21–3); another was the demand for simpler test procedures (see page 17–18).

Assessment and testing

The reliance placed on attainment targets and the testing and assessment of pupils at the key stages of 7, 11, 14 and 16 made this part of the Education Reform Act of great and controversial interest to those inside the education system. Testing and assessment were to be the public and visible way of enforcing the new curriculum.

It was a prime aim of the Act to make schools more account-able and give parents more and better information about their children's progress. Experience in the United States and elsewhere had shown the likelihood that the curriculum could become 'test-driven' if universal external testing were intro-duced in a simplistic or clumsy way. The English folk memory returned to Matthew Arnold's strictures on 'payment by results' and the three decades which followed the introduction of the New Code in 1862, spent in dismantling the disincentives to good teaching which that powerful administrative device instituted.

Teaching to the tests was a likely enough expectation. The question was: could sufficiently good tests be created to ensure that teachers who taught to them would do a good job?

Assessment is clearly an essential part of the teacher's job, and teachers regularly use standardised tests to help them. What sort of national scheme could be set up which would build on the best practice and make it the norm? How could it be ensured that assessment would avoid an excessive concentration on pencil and paper tests of a traditional kind?

The task of drawing up the outline of an assessment scheme fell to a group headed by Professor Paul Black of King's College, London, a scientist with considerable experience as a curriculum developer. His Task Group on Assessment and Testing (TGAT) produced a report at Christmas 1987 which became the basis of DES policy and a guide for the national curriculum subject working groups set up to consider attainment targets, pro-grammes of study and assessment arrangements. The TGAT report was accepted with alacrity by Mr Kenneth Baker and became the basis on which the attainment targets, programmes of study and assessment arrangements went forward over the next three and a half years. It is important, therefore, to describe the approach devised by Professor Black and his colleagues because of its influence on the course of events. But in 1990–91, Ministers became markedly less happy about the TGAT model and the elaborate assessment measures. By mid-summer 1991, DES support for TGAT had evaporated and the Government had come to favour simpler methods.

The scheme put forward by the Black Committee – generally known at the TGAT Report – envisaged a system of 'formative' assessment drawing heavily on teachers' observations as well as on 'standard assessment tasks' and other tests. The 'standard assessment tasks' could take the form of defined activity which was part of the normal teaching programme. In primary schools, the report suggested, children could undertake an assessment task without necessarily knowing it was a test which would be moderated and form part of graded assessment.

The aim, according to TGAT, had to be to produce 'a full and well-articulated picture of the individual child's current strengths and future needs'. It was essential to build on good classroom practice:

> 'A system which was not closely linked to normal classroom assignments and which did not demand the professional skills and commitment of the teachers might be less expensive and simpler to implement but would be indefensible in that it could set in opposition the processes of learning, teaching and assessment.'

This last is the key sentence in the report: it is all about trying to construct a *system* of assessment which runs in parallel with teaching and learning, and yet can be 'moderated' and 'standardised' to produce information about individual, class, school and local authority performance which can be usefully presented to parents and other 'consumers' teachers, administrators. . . .

TGAT assumed that the attainment targets which the Act required to be established for each subject would be divided up into groups, each group representing a different dimension of the subject. These groups of attainment targets would form what the TGAT report called the 'profile components'. These components ('preferably no more than four and never more than six') would reflect 'the variety of knowledge, skills and understanding to which the subject gives rise'.

The assessments would be based on these profile components and would include the teachers' own estimates, based on classwork, as well as the performance of the pupils on 'standard assessment tasks' and in tests. Development which would have to be undertaken before the system could be introduced would include the creation of an item bank of test questions to be administered by teachers in connection with their teaching. An important assumption, especially at the primary level, was that there would be considerable overlap of profile components, to reduce the number of separate assessments which individual teachers would be called upon to make, and to take account of cross-curricular themes.

The assessment of the various subject components would then be put together to form the complete assessment of the pupils' progress.

TGAT was anxious to devise a form of assessment which emphasised progression, and therefore constructed a framework of ten levels through which a pupil might be expected to climb.

At age 7 most (80 per cent) of pupils would achieve levels 1, 2 or 3 according to their assessed performance: 'Two years of learning represents one level of progress.' At age 11, 80 per cent would achieve levels 3 to 5. At age 14, the range would cover levels 4 to 7 and at age 16 there would be an overlap with the GCSE – levels 7 and 10 would, as the report put it 'bear some relationship to upper GCSE grades'.

This ingenious scheme was intended to prevent pupils from moving through the various assessment points with a static or scarcely changing mark or grade. It would provide a sense of progression. It would also enable the wide spread of achievement in each age-group to be accommodated by the use of levels below or above the national average. The form of assessment would be criterion-referenced (that is, expressed as far as possible in terms of specified tasks) and directly linked to the programmes of study laid down in the national curriculum, thereby providing a flexible scheme with testing at more or less fixed ages which would nevertheless do justice to children of all performance standards.

How the results were to be reported outside the school was a matter of widespread concern. TGAT made a number of sensible recommendations.

Assessment results for *individual* pupils should be confidential to pupils, their parents and teachers.

'The only form on which results . . . for . . . a given school should be published is as part of a broader report by that school of its work as a whole.'

The group rejected the idea of 'scaling' results up or down to take account of social factors. It recommended that 'national assessment results for a class as a whole and a school should be available to the parents of its pupils'.

Much concern had been expressed about the impact of formal national assessment and testing on the primary schools. TGAT favoured starting the tests at age 7 to identify at an early stage any who were under-performing, but wished to restrict the number of standard assessment tasks at age 7 to three, each task being designed to give 'systematic assessment of competence in the range of profile components appropriate to age 7'. It opposed any requirement for the publication of school results for 7-year-olds.

By the time they reached the age of 11, TGAT assumed that children would need to be assessed on three or four standard tasks which covered a range of profile components, 'possibly supplemented by more narrowly focused tests for particular components'.

The report emphasised (as such reports usually do) that its recommendations had to be considered as a whole – including the far-reaching sections on in-service training, research and development, and resources in time and materials. The time-table attached to the report provided for a five-year run-in period in which the assessment procedures and the curriculum development would go hand-in-hand, with the first full reporting of the results in year 5, in 1993.

The TGAT report was produced in five months – a feat in itself. It was an extremely skilful document in that it met the Secretary of State's requirement for an assessment scheme which would satisfy the provisions of the Education Reform Act, while at the same time it won the confidence of many teachers who had been sceptical or hostile to the idea of universal testing and assessment. This in itself was enough to arouse suspicions in certain Government quarters that the Group had subverted the radical intentions of the Act. A leaked letter from the Prime Minister's private office reported early doubts about the 'enormously elaborate and complex system' and the philosophy behind the scheme for formative and diagnostic rather than summative assessment. The central importance which the report placed on the role and judgments of teachers was also queried, along with the 'major role envisaged for the LEAs'. There were also doubts about the cost and the long lead time to bring the assessment and testing procedures into operation (*TES*, 18 March 1988).

These doubts appeared to be more muted as the Bill moved relentlessly forward to become an Act. It looked as if an attempt would be made, at some point, to simplify the working of the scheme and meet practical difficulties which might arise in its application. An assessment and testing scheme introduced in Croydon, independently of the Education Reform Act, appeared to produce a somewhat simpler method which might be expected to be easier for parents and employers to come to grips with. But the Black Committee's proposals were the only national scheme on offer and, from the DES point of view, there was clearly a great deal to be said for mobilising the widest possible support behind a scheme which would stand or fall on the cooperation of teachers.

The essential features of the scheme which the TGAT report combined were:

● close interdependence between curriculum, teaching and assessment;
● full involvement of teachers;
● varied forms of assessment, including assessment via tasks which form a normal part of classroom activity;
● time for the development of assessment measures and for the training of teachers in their use;
● assessment at the primary level which was compatible with good primary practice;
● sensible ground rules for reporting results;
● a realistic timetable for the introduction of the scheme.

The Government's formal response to the TGAT report came in a parliamentary answer (Hansard, 7 June 1988) which set out the main principles on which assessment would be based:

'(*a*) attainment targets will be set which establish what children should normally be expected to know, understand and be able to do at the ages of 7, 11, 14 and 16; these will enable the progress of each child to be measured against national standards.

(*b*) pupil's performance in relation to attainment targets should be assessed and reported on at ages 7, 11, 14 and 16. Attainment targets should be grouped for this purpose to make the assessment and reporting manageable.

(*c*) different *levels* of attainment and overall pupil progress demonstrated by tests and assessment should be registered on a ten-point scale covering all the years of compulsory schooling.

(*d*) assessment should be by a combination of national external tests and assessment by teachers. At age 16 the GCSE will be the main form of assessment, especially in the core subjects of English, mathematics and science.

(*e*) the results of tests and other assessments should be used both *formatively* to help better teaching and to inform decisions about next steps for a pupil, and *summatively* at ages 7, 11, 14 and 16 to inform parents about their child's progress.

(*f*) detailed results of assessments of individual pupils should be given in full to parents, and the Government attaches great importance to the principle that these reports should be simple and clear. Individuals' results should not be published, but aggregated results at the ages of 11, 14 and 16 should be, so that the wider public can make informed judgements about attainment in a school or LEA. There should be no legal requirement for schools to publish such results for seven-year-olds, though it is strongly recommended that schools should do so.

(*g*) in order to safeguard standards, assessments made by teachers should be compared with the results of the national tests and the judgement of other teachers.'

The principles followed the general lines of the TGAT recommendations, with some significant differences in regard to the publication of results. TGAT wanted to insist that results should only be published within the context of a report on the work of the school as a whole. This proviso was ignored in the ministerial statement. The TGAT report was opposed to any requirement for the formal publication of results at age 7. The ministerial statement stopped short of making publication at seven compulsory, but added a strong recommendation that such results should be published, notwithstanding the TGAT's serious doubts about the usefulness of the comparisons to which this might give rise.

It was clear that the TGAT report and the principles it adumbrated were only a beginning. A great deal would depend on how the scheme was developed, at every stage – from the setting of the attainment targets and the selection of the profile components, to the presentation of the results in detail and in aggregate.

In December 1988, research and development contracts worth £6 million were awarded to consortia of examining, research and academic bodies, with educational publishers, to prepare materials and Standard Assessment Tasks for the introduction of assessment for 7-year-olds. In July 1989, contracts worth £14 million were awarded for the development of Standard Assessment Tasks in English, Welsh, Science, Mathematics and Design and Technology for 14-year-olds. An important statement from the Secondary Examinations and Assessment Council, in August 1989, made it clear that teachers' assessment would be subordinate to the testing based on SATs.

SATs were used with 7-year-olds in 1991 – the first year when all children were assessed. The exercise was judged to be a success. But because the procedures were new and time-consuming, there were widespread complaints from teachers about the amount of work involved, and the amount of teaching time which was pre-empted for the tests. No doubt many of the teething troubles would have been overcome in time, but by now the political wind had changed and Ministers had become suspicious of the TGAT approach and the sophistication which had been built into SATs. Complaints from teachers hastened the loss of Ministerial patience and, in a highly political speech to the Centre for Policy Studies, the Conservative think-tank (July 3, 1991), the Prime Minister, Mr John Major, made the simplification of testing and assessment into a campaign issue. 'It is early days – and I readily accept that we may not have got the process right yet. Where it is wrong we will change it . . . *We need to shift the emphasis towards shorter, standardised tests which the whole class can take at one time.*' (The emphasis is Mr Major's.)

Religious worship and education

Until the passing of the Education Reform Act 1988, the only compulsory subject had been 'religious instruction' required under Section 25(2) of the Education Act 1944. Religious instruction had become 'religious education', by a mutation which by-passed the law. Its meaning had broadened in line with the weakening of religious commitment in society and the increase in the school population of pupils belonging to religions other than Christianity.

When the first draft of the Bill was published, those who spoke for the Roman Catholics and the Anglicans saw the omission from the list of core and foundation subjects of teaching about religion as evidence of the slide towards secularism. The Roman Catholic Bishop of Leeds, the Most Reverend David Konstant, an outspoken critic of the Bill, argued that the proposals were 'seriously flawed' in a number of key aspects which in the long term could do 'grave damage to our educational system'. Religious education was to be 'relegated to a place where it may have to jockey with ten other subjects for a share of four periods a week' (*TES*, 2 October 1987).

The decision to reinforce the compulsory status of religious instruction under the 1944 Act by putting in a specific reminder that the 1944 Act rules still applied was the Government's first response to fears that the omission of religious education from the list of core and foundation subjects might signal its progressive marginalisation. For many months it was maintained that as RE was compulsory already, under the 1944 Act, there was no need to put it in the special category created for the ten compulsory subjects set out in Section 3. Moreover, because religious education is subject to the parent's right to withdraw a child on grounds of conscience or for any other reason, it was felt that it would be inappropriate to introduce this complication into the newly-prescribed list of subjects.

It was further noted that the content of the national curriculum was to be determined by the Secretary of State: the content of religious education, on the other hand, was laid down locally in 'Agreed Syllabuses' drawn up by the Churches and other relevant bodies in special conferences convened by the local authority. The Churches wanted the subject to get the prestige which would follow from inclusion within the prescribed list, without any loss in the degree of local control.

Eventually, the matter was settled by a late amendment in the House of Lords which invented a new term to go alongside 'core' and 'foundation'. Religious education was included in Section 2(1)(a) as part of the 'basic' curriculum, without being subject to the particular conditions attached to the core and the foundation.

Ministers and their officials had been taken aback by the vehemence of the feelings aroused on religious issues in the Bill. This is surprising, perhaps, in view of the history of the 1902 and 1944 Acts. But even the presence at the head of the DES of the editor of the Faber book *English History in Verse* did not endow a radical government with a historical perspective! The religious argument flared, not just about religious education, but also about the daily act of worship.

What had been intended to be a routine tidying-up of the law on the daily assembly became a matter of great interest, especially in the House of Lords. There was a practical need to remove the 1944 Act insistence that the act of worship should be at the start of the school day, a legal requirement which was widely disregarded in practice. It was also necessary to allow it to take place in separate groups within the schools instead of *en masse* – something the 1944 Act only allowed if the accommodation available prevented the school meeting as a whole.

The Bill as drafted made these necessary changes. But their Lordships refused to leave the matter there. A small group of enthusiastic peers was determined to insert into those sections of the Act relating to religious education and the act of worship, a requirement that both should be of a mainly 'Christian' character. They rightly pointed out that this had been taken for granted in 1944. Now, they thought, it needed to be spelled out. This was done in Sections 7(2) in regard to the act of worship and 8(3) in the matter of religious education. Both sections are hedged about with 'mainly' and 'broadly'; and the provisions for appeal to the Standing Advisory Councils on Religious Education, where heads feel a Christian service is inappropriate, provide for local sensitivities to be recognised.

The Churches began by being distinctly reluctant to amend the Bill in this way. The Bishop of London, who acted as the Churches' spokesman in the Lords, found it acutely embarrassing to be harried by a zealous group led by, among others, Lord Thorneycroft and Lady Cox. The doubts of the Churches may have had something to do with an apprehension that the Judges might have a field-day if these clauses ever came before them under the judicial review procedure.

To many it seemed paradoxical that the 'Christian' character of religious education and religious worship in schools was being restated and enshrined in law at a time when the school population was more 'multi-faith' than ever before. But it was seen as a paradox which the schools could live with. It seemed unlikely that the enforcement of the new law would be any more effective than had been the enforcement of compulsory religious instruction and worship in the 1944 Act.

In response to broader worries about the secular and utilitarian values which some churchmen regarded as dominating the new curriculum, the reference to the 'spiritual, moral, cultural, mental and physical' development of pupils, in Section 1(2)(a) was added to the draft Bill, in a direct echo of Section 7 of the Education Act 1944. The significance of the addition was minimal, but it was welcomed by the Churches.

The precise status of religious education under the Act is less important than the way schools tackle the subject. As is noted below in connection with the allocation of time to the national curriculum, it was acknowledged that the constraints on religious education as a timetabled subject would be severe, and that, like careers education and a range of social and personal skills, it would depend on the successful development of cross-curriculum themes pursued alongside the ten specified subjects.

For the Roman Catholic bishops, the national curriculum was open to other, wider, objections, as they showed in their published commentary (*The Education Reform Bill* Catholic Bishops Conference, 1988). Aided schools had hitherto

'enjoyed the right to determine the complete school curriculum in the light of their understanding that the educational process should serve and nurture the whole person. The proposed Bill takes away the right . . . In practice this means that the Secretary of State and his advisers have the last word on what shall be taught in Catholic schools even if this conflicts with the ideals and practice of Catholic education . . . Secular authorities with no professional competence in the matter . . . have ultimate control of the curriculum in Church schools.'

Applicability
The national curriculum is mandatory on all maintained schools – that is, county and voluntary schools, and the new category of grant-maintained schools. It does not have legal force in independent schools, though most independent schools will make sure they can satisfy parents that they offer it or something better. New independent schools seeking registration will have to bear this in mind. City technology colleges (see Chapter 8) will have to provide 'a broad curriculum with an emphasis on science and technology'. The national curriculum does not apply to them, though the discussion document on the curriculum issued before the Bill was published indicated that the Secretary of State would 'make adherence to the substance of the national curriculum' a condition of grant.

Key Stage 4 – the 14–16 age groups
The DES Consultative Paper on the national curriculum, issued in advance of the Bill, gave an illustrative example of how the timetable for the last two years of compulsory education might work out under the constraints imposed by the national curriculum. This showed the ten compulsory subjects occupying some 75–85 per cent of the available time, with no allowance for religious education, or for additional science or mathematics. Subsequently ministers drew back from this draft illustration and in commending the Bill to Parliament in the Second Reading debate, Mr Baker contented himself with saying: 'it is our belief that it will be difficult if not impossible for any school to provide the national curriculum in less than 70 per cent of the time available.' In reality, nobody could say in advance of the publication of 'programmes of study' how much time would be required.

The first draft of the Bill was amended to underline the refusal to specify any particular periods of time. Section 4(3) makes this an explicit denial. In this it is unusual, in that it spells out what the Secretary of State must *not* put in an Order, instead of what he must or may.

It was Mr John Macgregor, Baker's successor as Secretary of State, who, early in 1990, brought the practical difficulties of Key Stage 4 to the attention of the National Curriculum Council. Recognising the impossibility of getting a quart into a pint pot, he invited the NCC to consider compromises, such as the designation of half-subjects, to make room for Religious Education and the additional studies which some students would need to pursue. But the NCC remained firmly attached to the 10-subject model and none of its suggestions won the support of Macgregor's robust successor, Mr Kenneth Clarke.

In a speech to the North of England Conference in January 1991, Clarke rehearsed once again the Key Stage 4 problem and explained the changes which the Government was determined to introduce:

'. . . I share the view that in the past too many young people have tended to have had a rather narrow and unbalanced education. We know that too many 14 and 15 year-olds effectively drop out of science or stop studying a modern foreign language. That is not acceptable in a nation that lives by its brains and is part of the European Community. . .

'But we have to secure . . . breadth without sacrificing the depth that is needed to get higher standards for all pupils, especially the average and less able and especially in the core subjects . . . By 14, young people are beginning to look at what lies beyond compulsory schooling whether in work or further study. We must harness that sense of anticipation . . .

'. . . It is simply not possible to have both the 10-course set menu and . . . provision for RE . . . plus the a la carte selections for some. A decision has to be made that leans one way or the other. I have decided, and I have inclined towards more flexibility and choice for these older pupils, their parents and teachers.

'The 10 subjects of the National Curriculum will continue to be required by law to be taught to all pupils to the age of 14. The programmes of study and attainment targets for each of them will be obligatory for every pupil . . . by Parliamentary Order.

'. . . My conclusions are as follows. First, all pupils should take GCSE in the core subjects, English, mathematics and science . . . Secondly . . . all pupils must study technology and a modern foreign language at Key Stage 4. However, I do not consider that all should be required to study these subjects to GCSE or equivalent qualifications . . . There may be a case for courses which combine these subjects with others – for example business studies with French or technology with art. . . .'

Thus a new core has emerged for Key Stage 4, different from the one envisaged by Parliament in 1988. It consists of English, Mathematics, Science, Technology, a Modern Foreign Language and some Physical Education. In addition, pupils will be required to do:

– a full course in History or a full course in Geography;
or
– a shorter course in both these subjects.

Abler pupils may do GCSE in both. Art and Music become options at Key Stage 4.

Other significant changes signalled in 1990–91, included the intention to offer a choice of explicitly pre-vocational courses from 14 onwards.

Special educational needs

There was considerable anxiety among those directly concerned with children with special educational needs that their interests might be prejudiced by the introduction of a national curriculum. At various points the Act acknowledges these concerns. Children with special needs are entitled to receive the national curriculum. Those who have been the subject of Statements (under Section 7 of the 1981 Education Act) may be exempted from all or part of the stipulated programmes of study and assessment procedures. Other pupils with special needs (but who have not been Statemented) may be allowed to pursue a modified programme for limited periods, on conditions, set out in regulations.

The Act is clearly not designed to make it easy for schools to take the line of least resistance with pupils who are failing to make the grade. The effect of the legal changes may be to put pressure on local authorities to provide 'statements' for more pupils, and for the needs of slow learners to be considered more carefully because the Act will only allow such children to be withdrawn from the regular course in prescribed circumstances.

Enforcement

The Education Reform Act set out the responsibilities of the local authorities and school governors for ensuring that the national curriculum is enforced. And the 1991 Education Bill reorganises Her Majesty's Inspectorate and requires all maintained schools to be inspected by accredited inspectors once every four years. Under the new provisions, the inspection reports will have to be published for parents together with plans for acting on the Inspectors' criticisms.

The local authorities will retain overall responsibility for monitoring standards, but will not be able to insist on using their own inspectors for this purpose; local authority inspectors (if accredited by HMI) will have to compete for inspection contracts alongside consultants from the private sector and from higher education.

In advance of the 1991 Bill becoming an Act, local authority inspectors and advisors have played a leading part in introducing the national curriculum and in providing the in-service training needed to support it. It remains to be seen what professional staff they will continue to need after inspection has been 'privatised', in order to evaluate the reports of accredited inspection teams, and to provide governors with the expert help which they need in matters of staff discipline and appraisal.

In addition to the monitoring functions undertaken by the local authority, direct intervention by parents is made possible through the complaints procedure. In terms of a market ideology, this gives the consumers (i.e. the parents, who throughout the Act are seen as surrogate consumers for their sons and daughters) a chance to act if they believe there is a failure to deliver the curriculum to which they are, by law, entitled. In an ideal market system, pressure by consumers would be all-important. Under the Act it seems unlikely to be of paramount significance, but dissatisfied parents who might otherwise feel impotent are given a weapon with which to fight back. It may also open up opportunities for barrack-room lawyers. Its main significance is likely to be to keep heads and their staff, and governing bodies, on permanent guard against the possibility of local challenge. They will watch their flanks with caution.

Action

The national curriculum requires action from the Secretary of State, from the local authorities, from governors, from head-teachers and their staff, and from parents.

The Secretary of State must activate the machinery to produce the programmes of study, attainment targets and procedures for testing and assessment. This means setting up working groups to prepare the programmes of study and attainment targets, sub-ject by subject, for the ten-subject curriculum laid down in Section 3 of the Act. He must set up and keep in being a National Curriculum Council and a School Examinations and Assessment Council. His proposals for the curriculum must be referred to the National Curriculum Council, starting with those for the core subjects. After receiving the advice of the Council (which must consult widely), he must then make up his own mind. If he rejects the advice, he must say why. Finally, he must incorporate his decision in Orders which have to be approved by both Houses of Parliament.

It then becomes the continuing duty of the curriculum and examinations councils to keep the national curriculum under review. The councils must advise on matters referred to them by the Secretary of State; they also have the right to give advice without waiting to be asked.

The timetable for the phased introduction of the national curriculum was set out in *National Curriculum: From Policy to Practice*. (DES 1989):

Timetable for implementing foundation subjects 1989/90–1996/97

SCHOOL YEAR	MATHEMATICS SCIENCE	DESIGN AND TECHNOLOGY	ENGLISH	(Provisional) GEOGRAPHY HISTORY	(Provisional) MODERN LANGUAGES MUSIC ART PHYSICAL EDUCATION
Autumn 1989 Summer 1990	KS1 – AT/PoS KS3 – AT/PoS		KS1 – AT/PoS		
Autumn 1990 Summer 1991	KS2 – AT/PoS KS1 – SAT¹	KS1 – AT/PoS KS2 – AT/PoS KS3 – AT/PoS	KS2 – AT/PoS KS3 – AT/PoS KS1 – SAT¹		
Autumn 1991 Summer 1992	KS1 – SAT² KS3 – SAT¹	KS1 – SAT¹	KS1 – SAT²	KS1 – AT/PoS KS2 – AT/PoS KS3 – AT/PoS	
Autumn 1992 Summer 1993	KS4 – AT/PoS KS3 – SAT²	KS1 – SAT² KS3 – SAT¹	KS4 – AT/PoS KS3 – SAT¹	KS1 – SAT¹	KS1 – AT/PoS KS2 – AT/PoS KS3 – AT/PoS
Autumn 1993 Summer 1994	KS2 – SAT¹ KS4 – GCSE/SAT	KS4 – AT/PoS KS2 – SAT¹ KS3 – SAT²	KS2 – SAT¹ KS3 – SAT² KS4 – GCSE/SAT	KS1 – SAT² KS3 – SAT¹	KS1 – SAT¹
Autumn 1994 Summer 1995	KS2 – SAT²	KS2 – SAT² KS4 – GCSE/SAT	KS2 – SAT²	KS4 – AT/PoS KS2 – SAT¹ KS3 – SAT²	KS1 – SAT² KS3 – SAT¹
Autumn 1995 Summer 1996				KS2 – SAT² KS4 – GCSE/SAT	KS4 – AT/PoS KS2 – SAT¹ KS3 – SAT²
Autumn 1996 Summer 1997					KS2 – SAT² KS4 – GCSE/SAT

KS=Key stage   SAT¹=**Unreported** assessment   SAT²=**First reported** assessment

AT/PoS=Statutory attainment targets and programmes of study take effect in the **first year** of the key stage shown

Timetable for implementing core subjects and design and technology 1989/90–1994/95

Pupil year at school	Pupil age	Key stage	School year 1989/90	School year 1990/91	School year 1991/92	School year 1992/93	School year 1993/94	School year 1994/95
1	5/6	**1**	MSE	MSET	MSET	MSET	MSET	MSET
2	6/7	SAT		M[1]S[1]E[1]	M[2]S[2]E[2]T[1]	MSET[2]	MSET	MSET
3	7/8			MSET	MSET	MSET	MSET	MSET
4	8/9				MSET	MSET	MSET	MSET
5	9/10	**2**				MSET	MSET	MSET
6	10/11	SAT					M[1]S[1]E[1]T[1]	M[2]S[2]E[2]T[2]
7	11/12	**3**	MS	MSET	MSET	MSET	MSET	MSET
8	12/13			MS	MSET	MSET	MSET	MSET
9	13/14	SAT			M[1]S[1]	M[2]S[2]E[1]T[1]	MSE[2]T[2]	MSET
10	14/15	**4**				MSE	MSET	MSET
11	15/16	GCSE/ SAT					MSE	MSET

M = Mathematics attainment targets and programmes of study in place
S = Science attainment targets and programmes of study in place
E = English attainment targets and programmes of study in place
T = Design and technology attainment targets and programmes of study in place
1 = **Unreported** assessment
2 = **First reported** assessment

Local education authorities must implement the national curriculum (Sections 1 and 10) and have regard to it in undertaking their statutory duties. Under the 1986 Act, they must 'make, and keep up to date' a written statement of their curriculum policy.

How much initiative a local authority retains in regard to curriculum policy also depends on the working out of other parts of the Act (in particular those on financial delegation – see Chapter 3). In practice, it will mainly be through monitoring school performance and through in-service training and local authority support services that the local authority will be able to give expression to its own curriculum policy. There will also be the chance to take up or reject opportunities offered by government initiatives by way of in-service training grants, Education Support Grants and Department of Employment programmes.

Governing bodies are (under the 1986 Act) responsible for the oversight of the curriculum at the school level and they must produce (and keep up to date) a curriculum policy document for parents, to show how they intend to meet the requirements of the national curriculum in the light of the local education authority's curriculum policy.

They have specific responsibility with regard to sex education, which they have discretion to include in the curriculum or exclude; and they have the obligation to ensure that, if it is included, it is 'given in such a manner as to encourage those pupils to have due regard to moral considerations and family life'. They are also bound by the local authority's duty not to 'promote' homosexuality, intentionally, nor to present homosexual relationships as an acceptable form of family life.

Headteachers must see that the national curriculum policy is carried out. Schools will have to take the programmes of study which emerge from the Curriculum Councils and turn them into syllabuses and working timetables. The attainment targets will form the framework within which these syllabuses will have to be fitted together.

It will be for the schools to work out how the 'subjects' of the national curriculum are to be taught and to interpret them alongside the other demands made on them for the teaching of themes which stretch across the curriculum. Similarly, it will be for the schools to decide whether their statutory obligations are better met by strict timetabling of compulsory subjects or by modular programmes which cover the ground in other ways.

In the case of grant-maintained schools (see Chapter 4) governing bodies and heads will have the same obligation to implement the national curriculum, but they will not have to have regard to the local authority's policy.

Parents are intended under the Act to become more discriminating consumers, watching school results, as published, and interpreting these results as best they can in the light of local circumstances. The assumption is that they will keep schools up to the mark by making their approval or disapproval known in informal contacts with governors and teachers, and through their formal opportunity to raise points (and pass resolutions) at the annual parents' meeting required by the 1986 Act. If complaints remain unanswered, parents can use the complaints procedure to force the school to deliver the national curriculum, or to force the local authority to use its powers to this end. If unable to get satisfaction, they can appeal to the Secretary of State. And, ultimately, parents have the power to remove their children from one school and send them to another. The procedures for doing so have been made marginally easier by the sections of the Act dealing with open enrolment, to which we now turn.

2

Open Enrolment

Sections 26 to 32: The admission of pupils to county and voluntary schools

The main aim behind these provisions was to increase significantly the power of parents as consumers. This was to be done by giving them a stronger say in which school their children should attend. To this end, it was decided to ensure that all maintained schools should accept a full complement of pupils up to the limit of their physical capacity, subject to as few exceptions as possible.

For each school there is a 'standard number' of places, the standard number being defined in section 15 of the 1980 Education Act, which took the 1979 entry number as the baseline and provided for ways of calculating the number for schools built or altered after that date.

Section 26 lays down that the authority responsible for admissions at any county or voluntary school may not as a general rule fix an admission limit lower than the relevant standard number.

ADMISSION OF PUPILS TO COUNTY AND VOLUNTARY SCHOOLS

26.—(1) The authority responsible for determining the arrangements for the admission of pupils to any county or voluntary school shall not fix as the number of pupils in any relevant age group it is intended to admit to the school in any school year a number which is less than the relevant standard number....

(3) Notwithstanding any provision of the articles of government of the school, ... the authority responsible for determining the arrangements for the admission of pupils to any such school may fix as the number of pupils in any relevant age group it is intended to admit to the school in any school year a number which exceeds the relevant standard number.

(4) A proposal may be made in accordance with the following provisions of this section for fixing as the number of pupils in any

such age group it is intended to admit to any such school in any school year a number which exceeds both—

    (a) the relevant standard number; and

    (b) any number fixed or proposed to be fixed for that purpose by the authority responsible for determining the arrangements for admission of pupils to the school.

(5) The proposal may be made—

    (a) where the authority responsible for determining those arrangements is the local education authority, by the governing body of the school; and

    (b) where that authority is the governing body of the school, by the local education authority....

(9) For the purposes of section 6(3)(a) of the 1980 Act (which exludes the duty to comply with a parent's preference as to the school at which education is to be provided for his child if compliance with the preference would prejudice the provision of efficient education or the efficient use of resources), no such prejudice shall be taken to arise from the admission to a school in any school year of a number of pupils in any relevant age group which does not exceed—

    (a) the relevant standard number; or

    (b) the number fixed in accordance with this section as the number of pupils in that age group it is intended to admit to the school in that school year;
    whichever is the greater....

It goes on to outline ways in which the standard number can be increased when this is not contested, and also in cases where a proposal for an increase is opposed and the issue has to go to the Secretary of State for a ruling.

The provision in the Education Act of 1944 (echoed in the 1980 Act) which subordinated parental preference to the provision of efficient education and the efficient use of resources is swept away (Section 26 (9)). Efficiency and economy are no longer relevant criteria. The particular circumstances of Church schools are taken into account in Section 30. Standard numbers in Aided schools are agreed between the governors and the local authority. If they cannot agree, the Secretary of State decides. The aim is to preserve the 'character' of the school. The 'selective' character of selective schools is also unchanged.

Having established the enlarged right of parents to get their children into the schools of their choice up to the physical limit of the capacity of the available buildings, the Act goes on to set out other ways in which the standard number may be varied. Section 27(5) and (6) cover cases where the local authority judges it necessary to apply to the Secretary of State for an order reducing the standard number, and Section 28 sets out the procedure to be followed in making and dealing with such an application, including the publication of notices and the consideration of objections, along similar lines to the procedure for dealing with a change of a school's character or use.

Section 28(7) defines the circumstances in which the Secretary of State can make an order reducing the standard number. He can only do this on the narrow grounds set out in Section 28(7): this states that the *only* relevant consideration is the physical capacity of the school buildings. He cannot approve an application 'unless he is satisfied that the reduction is necessary, having regard to any reduction in the school's capacity' as compared with its capacity when the standard number was fixed – if, for example, accommodation has been taken out of use.

The standard numbers for primary schools (Section 29) are defined in a form which includes the 'rising fives' – children aged between four years and six months and five years old. This removes an anomaly created by the 1980 Act whereby a school's standard number might bear little relation to the actual number of pupils in the reception class in the year in question.

28.—(1) Where the authority responsible for determining the arrangements for the admission of pupils to any county or voluntary school intend to apply to the Secretary of State for an order ... reducing any standard number applying to the school ... they shall publish their proposals with respect to the reduction in such manner as may be required by regulations made by the Secretary of State and submit to him a copy of the published proposals together with their application.

Background

Open enrolment was promised in the Conservative election manifesto for the General Election, published in May 1987.

This included the following promise:

'Schools will be required to enrol up to the school's agreed physical capacity instead of artificially restricting pupil numbers, as can happen today. Popular schools, which have earned parental support by offering good education, will then be able to expand beyond present physical numbers.

'These steps will compel schools to respond to the views of parents.'

The reasoning behind the proposal was beguilingly simple. The Government wanted to put parents into a stronger position in relation to the education system. In part this sprang from populist rhetoric: the analysis of the defects of the present education system which ministers had adopted, attributed many weaknesses to what Mr Baker called the dominance of the producers. Giving more power to the consumers was a logical way to reduce that dominance. There was also the true perception that parents' encouragement and support were prime ingredients in successful education. Giving parents more power of choice could be a potent way of conscripting their commitment.

Beyond this, there was the ideological belief that education could get some of the benefits of a competitive market if consumers had more power to influence the producers by showing, actively, their preference for one school and one kind of education over another.

Giving parents an unrestricted right of access for their children to the school of their choice, till the last desk in that school was filled, was the way chosen to project these aims at the local level.

To gauge the impact of the change, we have to put these proposals in the perspective of earlier legislation. Under an Act of Parliament passed in 1980 (also brought forward by a government headed by Mrs Thatcher) the arrangements for the allocation of pupils to schools set out in the 1944 Act were revised. The context in which this took place was much affected by falling rolls – the working out in primary and secondary schools of the fall in the birthrate between 1964 and 1977.

Demography always has a bearing on educational planning and administration – usually a bigger part than ideology. For thirty years, the education system was driven forward on the tide of expansion and the energy and the optimism which this evoked. After the mid-1970s it was the problems raised by a lengthy period of contraction which came to dominate planning:

the need to cope with a demographic trend which reflected a fall in the school population of nearly one-third – 3 million pupils – from the height of the boom to the depth of the slump.

Falling rolls meant surplus school places unless or until schools were reorganised to take places out of service. At the time of the 1980 Act, two parallel policies were adopted. The first policy was to reduce the provision. This went forward, unevenly throughout the country. Local education authorities, in the main, kept up with, or exceeded, the targets set by the Government for the elimination of empty classrooms, through the closure and merger of schools and by the taking out of service of surplus buildings. By the time the Education Reform Bill was published in 1987, more than 1.25 million places had been eliminated.

It was, however, clearly recognised that it would never be practicable to take out all surplus places as fast as pupil numbers declined – nor yet that, given the uncertainty of all demographic forecasting, it would be sensible to try to do so. The expectation had to be that, even if local authorities were prudent in reducing their stock of school buildings, it would still be necessary to manage a system in which there were more school places than pupils to fill them.

The second policy, therefore, was to give authorities more discretion over the number of pupils to be admitted to each school. This meant addressing the emotive question of how much choice parents should have in the matter of the placement of their children.

The 1944 Act had established parents' rights to express a preference about the schools their child should attend. Section 76 did this in the form of a grand declaratory but far from definitive expression of good intentions:

'In the exercise and performance of all powers and duties conferred and imposed on them by this Act, the Secretary of State and the local education authorities shall have regard to the general principle that so far as is compatible with the provision of efficient instruction and training and the avoidance of unreasonable public expenditure, pupils are to be educated in accordance with the wishes of their parents.'

In practice, this was of limited use, though no doubt it helped to shape the policy of local authorities in the great majority of uncontentious cases. It did not prevent authorities most of the time treating each case on its educational and administrative merits. Parent's wishes were to be taken into account, but not treated as sovereign.

When confrontation did arise, however, certain defects in administering the 1944 Act became apparent because the really persistent parent, who was prepared to keep his child out of school long enough to force the authority to prosecute, could usually get his own way in the end, even if the school of his choice was, technically, full up. Isolated cases of this nature were an irritation which exposed the inadequacy of the law and its enforcement.

The 1980 Act, therefore, set out to reform the procedure. The parents' right to choose (or, rather, express a preference which the local education authority had to take into account) was again guaranteed and local appeals committees were created to deal with disputed cases. And arrangements for the serving of school attendance orders were tightened up to remove the loophole by which stubborn parents had been able to frustrate the purpose of proceedings.

The most important sections of the 1980 Act, however, concerned the way of deciding how many pupils a school should be required to admit. Each school was given a 'standard number', based on the 1979–80 entry. But the local authority was accorded the power to fix an admission limit, up to 20 per cent below this number, at its own discretion. An even lower limit could be fixed, but only after publishing proposals and submitting these to the Secretary of State for his approval.

The 1980 Act, then, ostensibly put parental rights of choice at the forefront, but in reality was a way of curbing them more effectively.

What the Education Reform Act did was sweep away the discretionary element which had allowed local authorities to set aside parents' wishes. It expressly rejected any suggestion that efficiency or economy (however phrased) could constitute a valid reason for refusing a parent's demand for a child to attend a particular school. The only considerations which were to be relevant were those which arose from the physical capacity of the school. This was spelled out: a Secretary of State who deviated from this in considering an application for a lower admissions number, would court an action for judicial review.

After 1980, many local authorities took the opportunity presented by falling rolls to reduce the size of their larger secondary schools, and schools got used to living in less crowded conditions. The space provision in many secondary schools built in the late 1960s and early 1970s was extremely tight; there were good reasons why teachers welcomed the easement which the 1980 Act made possible.

Local education authorities also used their power to control intake to prevent highly popular schools from becoming uncomfortably full while less popular schools became uneconomically and inefficiently small. Writing in *The Independent* soon after the Government's open enrolment proposals had been set out, Tim Brighouse, then Oxfordshire's County Education Officer, gave as examples of the way the 1980 Act had been used, two secondary schools in the Oxfordshire town of Witney. One was a former grammar school, the other a former secondary modern school. As he put it:

> 'The ex-grammar school was sometimes (wrongly) perceived by the public to have a better reputation. In fact both schools were equally successful academically. Had the 1980 Act not existed, one of these perfectly good schools might have been crippled by innuendo and rumour . . . the other school would have become painfully overcrowded. As it was, each school prospered. The now expanding town needs two schools and has two good ones.'

Similar examples could be quoted from all over the country.

Brighouse's example pinpointed the implications of open enrolment for local authority school planning. The local authority associations were highly critical of these sections of the Act because they believed it would make it harder for authorities to carry out their responsibilities under Section 8 of the 1944 Education Act: to maintain 'sufficient' schools, suitable for the purposes required, to provide for all children in their areas. Their concern was that if market forces took over from rational planning, in deciding which schools should survive and which be closed, the task of the local authorities would change to a marked degree and it would become much harder for them to fulfil their statutory duties within the resources available to them. Some of these fears were echoed in statements from the Audit Commission, which maintained a continuing interest in the elimination of surplus school accommodation and the financial savings which would follow from energetic closure policies.

The Education Reform Act, as it stands, however, does nothing to make the continued retention of surplus accommodation any easier. Taken together, open enrolment and financial delegation (see Chapter 3) may be thought to accentuate the pressure on local education authorities to be active managers of their capital. Because financial delegation will fund schools through formulae which are based on per capita payments (suitably weighted for other relevant factors), schools which are popular and recruit more pupils automatically get more money and resources. By the same token, schools which lose pupils and fail to recruit a full complement, quickly lose money and resources. The effect is, therefore, to speed up the process of attrition which makes unpopular schools unviable and forces local authorities to embark on schemes of reorganisation and closure. The Act recognises this need by drawing attention to the provision of Sections 12 and 13 of the 1980 Act which relate to closures and change of use.

The Act is not concerned with speculation about its wider impact, except in so far as it limits the circumstances in which popular schools can extend beyond their standard number and specifies the routines they must go through if they wish to change their character – for instance, if they become so popular as to wish to become selective.

The competitive exercise is likely to foster large schools: but large schools are not necessarily the best or the most popular, so it could be that open enrolment might turn out to have within it a self-correcting mechanism.

These matters were of concern to the voluntary school authorities as well as the local education authorities. The Roman Catholic bishops raised doubts about open enrolment on two grounds. (*The Education Reform Bill* Catholic Bishops Conference, 1988). The first was a general anxiety that the character of their schools might be changed if they were obliged to recruit non-Catholic children up to the physical capacity of the schools. They did not believe that the safeguards in the first draft of the Bill were strong enough. The exemptions in the 1980 Act which applied where there were agreements between the voluntary school and the local authority were retained, but the bishops observed that 'such agreements are not always in existence, nor always enforceable'.

Secondly, the bishops objected to open enrolment on the grounds that it might cause them additional expense if they were obliged to maintain more physical plant than was needed. Though the second objection was expressed in financial terms, it was an indirect way of drawing attention again to the planning consequences of open enrolment.

Their objections were met by the inclusion of Section 30, which spelled out the need for an agreement between the governors and the LEA, with the aim of preserving the school's character.

Competition

Open enrolment has the effect of stepping up competition in recruitment between schools.

Even before the passing of the Act, falling rolls had forced schools to compete for clients. Those that failed to attract their share of applicants knew that sooner or later their viability would be called in question. The 1988 Act accentuated these competitive pressures. The result has been to give much greater importance to public relations. Schools have now to present themselves in the most favourable light by means not hitherto used. It was one of the main aims behind the Act to force schools to be more responsive to parents and more attentive to their wishes. Open enrolment looks like an effective way of forcing schools to market themselves with more zeal than ever before.

Wise parental choice depends on a good flow of relevant information about the methods of operation of admissions procedures, about schools' internal organisation and policy, about disciplinary methods and curriculum policies. Parents are now entitled to be kept informed on all these matters as a result of the

Education Acts of 1980 and 1986, and the Education Reform Act of 1988.

In future, the statutory requirements for information would be reinforced by competition for pupils, stimulated by open enrolment which would provide a powerful, market-driven incentive for a new and open approach to parents.

Reference has already been made to the requirements laid down in connection with the national curriculum (see Chapter 1) to publish the results of the testing and assessment procedures to which children are submitted at ages 7, 11, 14 and 16. Other external examination results must also be available to parents. For many, these results form the best evidence on which to compare performance, because they show the results of one school in a form which can immediately be put alongside those of another.

Nothing succeeds like success or fails like failure. If enough people were to come to the conclusion that school A was better than school B, and back their judgement by sending their children to school A, they would soon be vindicated. School B would go out of business and school A would show all the outward signs of success – at least in the short term.

A lot of attention has focused on the *interpretation* of the results of examinations, because these are only valid indicators if like is being compared with like. It is notoriously difficult to make fair comparisons between the performance of schools, because the quality of the education (as opposed to the examination results) depends on the quality of the inputs as well as the outcomes. The work of the teachers is one of the inputs. The potential of the pupils is another. A true comparison, therefore, inevitably turns on the qualities the pupils bring to school with them, as well as the skill of the teachers and the efficiency of the school organisation. Pupil potential varies widely between schools and seems to relate to external social factors.

Inevitably, in the circumstances, governors and teachers face professional and ethical questions of a high order in deciding how to present test and examination results in such a way as to show their school in the most favourable light, while at the same time being strictly fair and responsible. Fairness and keen competition are not always easy bedfellows. The Act itself is silent on how they should be reconciled, except in a negative sense: there is an obligation to publish, but nothing on how the crude results should be put in perspective. It was left to local authorities to issue their own voluntary guidelines if they thought fit.

As we have seen, the Secretary of State's reaction to the TGAT report (Chapter 1) offered no guidance on how to avoid giving parents a misleading impression. He was concerned to emphasise the obligation to provide parents with the results of their own individual children, and to publish 'aggregated' scores at ages 11, 14 and 16, so that the wider public could make 'informed judgments' about attainment in a school or LEA. He also stressed the importance of providing reports which were 'simple and clear'. Unfortunately, it is doubtful if there is any 'simple and clear' way of presenting the complex information necessary to make an 'informed judgment' of the kind he has asked for.

Detailed guidance on the Open Enrolment sections of the Act was set out in Circular 11/88 – *Admission of pupils to county and voluntary schools.* In the first phase, open enrolment applied to Secondary schools. Circular 6/91 – *More Open Enrolment: Extension to Primary Schools* marked the second stage in the implementation of the Act.

3

Finance and Staff

Sections 33 to 51

These sections cover two main topics: the delegation of financial responsibility from local authorities to their schools; and matters relating to the appointment, suspension and dismissal of staff in local authority maintained schools.

The delegation of financial responsibility goes by various names. The Act refers to 'financial delegation'. Local authority experimental schemes used the term 'local financial management' (LFM). The DES consultants, Coopers and Lybrand, coined the term 'local school management' to make this wider managerial emphasis even more explicit, and LMS is what the Department has used in its official guidance on the matter.

In essence, the object of the changes in the law was to make local authorities distribute funds to the secondary schools and their larger (200 pupils and above) primary schools by means of a weighted, *per capita* formula. Governing bodies of these schools are to be made responsible for controlling the budgets thus delegated to them. The sections covering staff matters follow from the related desire to give governing bodies more control over appointments and the management decisions relating to staff.

Certain technical terms are used. The 'general schools budget' is the local authority's total spending on schools. The 'aggregated schools budget' is that part of the general schools budget which is to be distributed to schools under the delegation scheme. 'School's budget share' is the share of the aggregated school's budget, payable to an individual school, and placed under the management of the governing body.

Finance

Section 33 provides the Secretary of State with the power to require local education authorities to prepare schemes of financial delegation for county and voluntary schools.

Financing of schools maintained by local education authorities
33.—(1) It shall be the duty of every local education authority to prepare a scheme in accordance with this Chapter and submit it for the approval of the Secretary of State . . .

(2) The scheme shall provide for—

(a) the determination in respect of each financial year of the authority, for each school required to be covered by the scheme . . . of the share to be appropriated for that school . . . of the part of the general schools budget of the authority . . . which is available for allocation to individual schools . . . as the school's budget share; and

(b) the delegation by the authority of the management of a school's budget share for any year to the governing body of the school where such delegation is required or permitted by or under the scheme . . .

Section 34 goes into the detail of what local authorities have to do in preparing their plans. They have to get the approval of the Secretary of State before any scheme comes into force, and he can issue his own guidelines, either generally or in the case of particular authorities. Authorities must also consult the governors of every county and voluntary school. The Secretary of State can impose his own scheme if one satisfactory to him is not forthcoming.

In taking responsibility for spending the school's budget (Section 36), the governors are bound by their duty to ensure the national curriculum is taught and by rules of the scheme. They can delegate their own powers to the head (within the terms of the scheme) and cannot be held personally liable for anything done in good faith in the exercise of financial duties delegated to them or by them to the head.

Delegation can be suspended by the local authority if it believes the governors have been guilty of 'a substantial or persistent' failure to do their job, or are otherwise not doing it properly, by giving them one month's notice of suspension (Section 37). This power is hedged around with conditions which provide a right of appeal by the governors to the Secretary of State.

A crucial stage in the delegation procedure concerns the preparation of a formula for sharing out the 'aggregated budget' among the schools. This is covered in Section 38.

The distribution formula is to be based on the number of pupils, and may be weighted to take account of 'any other factors affecting the needs of individual schools which are subject to variation from school to school' (Section 38(3)(b)). In this connection, particular mention is made of pupils with special needs.

Certain elements in the local authority's total education budget may be excluded from the amount which is available for sharing out among schools through the formula. Section 38(4) provides for the exclusion of all capital items, all debt charges, all funds received under specific grants from the central government such as education support grants, and 'such other items of expenditure as may be prescribed'. Under the last category would come authority-wide support services like the psychological service, and such advisory and inspection services as were excluded from the approved scheme.

When a local authority's scheme has been approved by the Secretary of State it must be published. Section 42(1) provides for this and for the publication each year of detailed information about the funding of schools under the delegation scheme. Subsection 4 itemises what must be set down in the annual statement. This includes:

- the amount of the 'general schools budget'
- the amount of the 'aggregated schools budget'
- details of what heads of expenditure have *not* been included in the delegated funds
- details of the allocation formula
- school-by-school figures for expenditure per pupil
- details of the expenditure (expressed in per-pupil terms) in each school which is to be met by the local authority from its retained budget for excepted services.

Authorities must also publish a report at the end of each financial year giving the money spent on each school.

Financial delegation to special schools is separately covered in Section 43. Governors of special schools may be given delegated control over their budgets, but these budgets are fixed by local authorities at their own discretion, not according to a predetermined formula.

The last financial section – Section 50 – applies to schools which are *not* bound by financial delegation. Each is to be given once a year a financial statement covering the capital and current expenditure by the local education authority at the school. Each school is to have a capitation allowance to be spent at the discretion of the governors. The local authority's financial statement may be incorporated in the governors' annual report.

The financial delegation sections of the Act depend on Orders laid before Parliament by the Secretary of State. It is expected that schemes will be introduced over a period of several years, depending on local circumstances and the progress of negotiations on the funding formulae. Different dates might apply to different schools or categories of school. Local authorities are to submit their schemes by September 1989 and to implement them fully by April 1993. (Different dates apply to the new London education authorities.)

Staff

Appointments, suspensions and dismissals are covered in Section 44 and 45, and by rules set out in Schedule 3 of the Act. The powers of governors, already increased under the 1986 Act, are extended still further, with a corresponding reduction in the local authority's power to intervene. Under the 1986 Act, local authorities were given the right to establish a staff complement for each school. That power is withdrawn by the 1988 Act. The local education authority has remained the employer of the teachers, but all appointments are made by the governors. The chief education officer's role in senior appointments (heads and deputies) has been explicitly recognised – CEOs must give advice on these appointments and the governors must consider this. CEOs also advise on other appointments if asked. The local authority can only refuse to confirm an appointment made by the governors if the candidate fails to satisfy the Education (Teachers) Regulations 1982, as, for example, on grounds of doubt about health, conduct, or qualified status. Similar revised arrangements apply to appointments of staff of Aided schools.

If a member of staff at a maintained school is dismissed or retires prematurely, the cost is not to be met from the school's delegated budget, unless the local authority 'has good reason' to make the deduction. A 'no redundancy policy' is expressly ruled out as 'good reason' (Section 46(6)).

Background

On the surface, this was one of the most practical – and at the same time, least contentious – chapters in the Act. The idea of putting more decisions at the school level received general support. Yet behind the common sense were the outlines of even more radical changes and yet more controversy.

The legislation aimed to release powers of initiative which had hitherto been stifled by local bureaucracy. If this could be done, there would be a greater commitment from governors and from heads and their staff, and better value for money all round. There would also be the added advantage (in the eyes of the sponsors of the Bill) that enforced delegation would strip local authorities of the power to interfere politically in the running of the schools. In this sense, these sections of the Act belong to the continuing quarrel between a Conservative government and left-wing Labour education authorities.

Local financial management had, however, already begun to look like an idea whose time had come, before the Bill was drafted. Well publicised projects in Solihull and Cambridgeshire had shown what could be done to devolve budgetary control to governors and school staffs. Behind these pilot schemes were many more, less developed, innovations aimed at transferring more and more financial decisions to the schools. Although teachers were suspicious that some of the interest in financial delegation sprang from a desire among local politicians and administrators to pass the buck – to shift the odium attaching to difficult budgetary decisions – the experience in Cambridgeshire and Solihull had been that those who had taken part in such schemes welcomed the increased responsibility.

To some extent this was a matter of temperament and styles of headship. Some Cambridgeshire heads were more enthusiastic than others about adding to their managerial responsibilities. But for many who had complained in the past about the irksome nature of petty bureaucratic financial controls and how long it took to get minor services performed by the county authorities, the opportunity for a head to cut through the red tape and take decisions – working within a clear budget – was greatly appreciated.

There was another reason why the early experimental financial delegation schemes worked. The Cambridgeshire pilot scheme owed much of its popularity to a firm understanding between the participating schools and the county authority that any savings which local financial management might yield would be 'kept' by the school, not clawed back retrospectively by the county.

The initial budget of a school over which control was delegated was based on the school's previous budgetary history, not (as the Education Reform Act ordained) on a mechanical formula. So a school received a financial allocation based on its previous year's expenditure, adjusted for price changes and expected changes in pupil rolls. Given this 'historic' budget, the school could then so manage its affairs as to live within it. Any savings which it could make by, say, monitoring the heating or lighting more closely, could be used to increase spending on, say, ancillary services. And it could engage in this pursuit of candle-ends, confident in the knowledge that the county would give it a budget for the following year which would not be cut.

In truth, of course, such a gentleman's agreement between the pilot school and the county could never be permanent. Sooner or later, when money was specially tight, it would fall apart. But this lay in the future. The experimental schemes were a success; schools enjoyed tangible benefits and financial gains. Authorities were only beginning to wrestle with the practical difficulties of moving from historic costs to universal formulae when the Bill was announced.

The local authorities objected to the legal imposition of financial delegation but had difficulty in opposing it – after all, local authority models had provided the inspiration for the proposals – but they recognised that the mixture of motives behind the new legislation included a determination to reduce their own political and educational influence.

It is difficult to relate the various sections of the Act to each other without risk of repetition. The financial delegation provisions have a direct connection with those on open enrolment (Chapter 2) – because they effectively ensure that funding follows the pupil; and with grant-maintained schools (Chapter 4) – because they provide a mechanism for determining how much money the government can recoup from a local authority if one of its schools opts out.

The result is to create a situation in which the resources – i.e. *per capita* payments – which a school receives depend directly on the choices which parents exercise. The school has ceased to be 'maintained' as an institution independently of those choices. Under schemes of delegation the *per capita* payments are still paid to the school; but the circumstances have been engineered in which it would be a relatively simple matter to give the money directly to the parents instead – in the form of vouchers or warrants – thereby completing the transfer of power from the institutions and the local authority to the parents.

Though these possible future developments are outside the scope of the Education Reform Act 1988, they are certainly part of the background to the Act and the patterns of thought which lie behind it (see Chapter 10).

Attempts to devise a practical voucher scheme or voucher experiment failed in 1982–83 and by the time of the 1983 election the Secretary of State for Education, Sir Keith Joseph (now Lord Joseph), had formally shelved the idea, as had the Prime Minister. The pressure among the right-wing lobbies which campaigned for more choice, competition and market discipline in education did not relax, however. The 1988 Act marked their success in putting together a set of proposals which seemed attractive enough in their own right to form the basis of an election manifesto, while at the same time adapting the education system in such a way as to make a future transition to vouchers possible without undue disruption. Ministers, however, seemed more intent on advocating the expansion of the grant-maintained sector than in pushing the idea of vouchers (see page 176).

Local school management

The Act requires each authority to draw up its own scheme of financial delegation. This has to be submitted to the Secretary of State who must approve it before it can come into force. The procedure gives a good illustration of the way the Act has concentrated power in his hands. He can approve, disapprove or modify proposals put to him by an authority. Or he can put in his own scheme if an authority fails to meet his demands. He makes regulations which authorities must follow. The implementation of the policy was in two stages. The first stage was governed by Circular 7/88 (*Education Reform Act: Local Management of Schools*). In addition to the official guidelines, there was a report by consultants Coopers and Lybrand also entitled *Local Management of Schools*, which, though not endorsed in every particular as DES policy, was also to be regarded as a guide to action. Guidance for the second stage was set out in Circular 7/91 (see page 60).

Money was provided by means of Educational Support Grants to pay for small development teams in each local authority to work on schemes (an average of £300,000 an authority: £30 million in all) to cover work up to 1993. An average of £2,000 was set aside for each primary school, £4,500 for each secondary school, for Information Technology. A £65 million three-year package included five days training for each school.

The Act emphasises the need for each authority to consult with the governing bodies and heads of every one of its county and voluntary schools in preparing a scheme. This seems to suggest that schemes are to be adjusted carefully to local needs – even to the needs of each individual school. But how closely such a scheme can be tailored to the separate needs of each establishment is far from clear. Most of the attention in Parliament and outside was fixed on the less flexible elements of the legislation – the establishment of an 'aggregated schools budget' and the 'formula' to be used to split this global sum into the 'budgetary shares' of the individual schools.

Aggregated schools budget   To calculate this, the local authority must first take out those items from the 'general schools budget' which are to be 'excluded' and are to continue to be dealt with centrally by the authority.

First there are the items which are listed in the statute: capital expenditure, debt charges, and items covered by specific central government grants (like educational support grants and the in-service training grants). And secondly, there are the items which the Secretary of State has decided to keep out under the discretionary powers given him in Section 38(4)(d): central administration, inspectors/advisors and home-school transport.

Over and above this list of mandatory exclusions, the Circular discusses a number of other items which authorities may, if they so wish, propose to exclude when they submit their schemes for the Secretary of State's approval. These include:

- school meals
- child guidance and education welfare
- statemented pupils and special units
- peripatetic and advisory teachers
- structural repairs and maintenance
- pupil support
- certain staff costs: 'safeguarding' and cover.

Authorities had to hold back funds for contingencies and for emergencies, and for occasional staff expenses relating to dismissals and early retirements. It was possible for them to earmark funds for particular purposes – for example, a favoured curriculum development. Such money would be available for schools, but only for that particular purpose, and would not form part of the delegated budget. The possibility of such earmarked funding is recognised in Circular 7/88, but it is obvious that the more the exclusions and exceptions, the smaller the amount which remains for the schools' budget share. The DES guidance indicated that fixed limits would be imposed on the non-mandatory exceptions – that is, the items which local authorities may add to the initial list of exclusions laid down by the Act and by the Secretary of State. The Circular put an upper limit of 10 per cent on these exceptions, with the requirement of a further review within three years to bring the percentage down to 7.

The formula
Having worked out the proportion of total expenditure to be delegated to schools, local authorities have then to devise a formula for its distribution which gives proper weight to the varied (and variable) factors which reflect the needs of different schools.

The formula must apply to all schools, not just those which 'qualify' for financial delegation. Schools which were too small to qualify under Circular 7/88 still had to have a budget share, even though they were not in direct control of their budgets. The Act provides for the Secretary of State to lower the 'qualifying' figure by regulation if he thinks fit.

The funding of all the schools in a local authority area by means of a single formula is central to the strategy and ideology underlying the Act. It reduces the local authority's power to intervene in favour of one school rather than another, thereby limiting the scope for political intervention. It simplifies the introduction of grant-maintained schools (see Chapter 4) by providing a common basis for funding. And as we have seen, it represents a stepping-stone for a possible future move to vouchers.

The imposition of formula funding inevitably means that some schools are winners and some losers – historic costs reflect differences of treatment, some reasonable, some arbitrary, which have been established over a period of years. It has been necessary, therefore, to provide safety nets to ensure that no school should suffer too sharp a change in its funding as the result of Local Management. The formulae are meant to have an objective fairness built into them. In practice this is often more apparent than real.

There is an obvious ready comparison with the formulae used to calculate the Grant Related Expenditure Assessments which were used to construct the Rate Support Grant. These were meant to provide an objective way of grant-aiding local authorities, assuming a common standard of provision. In their complexity, they confounded those who had to use them, few of whom could say they fully understood the statistical basis for the eventual distribution of grant.

The Circular recognised this danger and insisted that the formulae should be 'simple, clear and predictable'. But, though simplicity is the ideal of every administrator at the outset, the circumstances which the formula must encompass are far from simple, and therein lies the irresistible tendency towards increasing complexity – or grosser forms of unfairness.

Some 70 per cent of a school's budget is likely to be devoted to teaching and non-teaching salaries and the 'costs of employment' like national insurance and superannuation. The DES guidance makes it clear that in addition to salary items, delegation is expected to extend to school's day-to-day premises costs, including rent and rates, and books, equipment and other goods and services.

The formula has to be so framed that it takes into account the fixed costs which schools have to meet, irrespective of minor changes in roll. It is not sufficient to provide a single *per capita* sum for all children: the formula must be sensitive not only to the age of the child but the size of the school and the stage of education. It will be open to the authority to weight its own assumptions about staffing, using its own curriculum-led staffing model. It will obviously be extremely hard to do this in such a way as to ensure that teaching the full national curriculum is possible in a school which has begun to lose pupils in the aftermath of open enrolment. Smaller schools will certainly need a bigger *per capita* payment than larger schools.

A great deal depends on how teachers' salaries are dealt with in the formula. The Government decided that there is to be no complement of teachers for each school laid down by the local authority. It is up to the governors to decide how many teachers, of what kind, to employ. But the Coopers and Lybrand report argued that difficulties would arise if some arrangement were not made to even out the cost of teachers at different points in the incremental scale.

The consultants proposed that instead of charging against each school's budget share the actual cost of the salaries of the teachers on the staff, the local authority should act as a staffing agency, bearing the cost of recruiting and supplying staff itself, and charging the schools a flat-rate cost.

Dr David Muffett, the chairman of the Hereford and Worcester education committee, and a well-known maverick Conservative local politician, took up the point in an article in *The Times Educational Supplement* on 19 August 1988. He compared the teachers' salary costs of all the ten-teacher primary schools in his county, and found that in the summer of 1987, these costs varied from £116,166 to £133,671 – a range of more than £17,500. Dr Muffett found this entirely unacceptable, and most local authority administrators would agree with him.

The effect of *not* providing some such balancing mechanism as the consultants proposed would be to put governors under pressure to replace older, more experienced and more expensive teachers with young men and women just out of college. Because of the significance of teachers' salaries within the school budget, they would have to tailor their staff selection criteria to these crude financial incentives. It was reasonable to ask if this was in the minds of ministers and members of parliament when the Act was passed.

The Coopers and Lybrand suggestion was rejected. The Circular acknowledges that the formula will have to take account of 'variations between the actual teaching costs of some small schools and the LEA's average costs of employing teachers'. This covers three-quarters of the schools. As a general principle, schemes will provide for the charging of 'actual sums (including actual pay)'.

In addition to the general and particular needs of small schools, the Circular makes special mention of two other factors to be taken into account in weighting the formula. One is the variation in costs of pupils with special needs; the other is the cost of sixth form provision, which may differ from subject to subject.

Further concessions on staffing costs were announced in August 1989 when the first local school management scheme (for Norfolk) was approved. Mrs Angela Rumbold, the Minister of State, said: 'We shall look sympathetically at proposals to extend the transition period selectively for schools which would otherwise be faced with annual reductions of one per cent or more in their total budgets because their staff costs are above the local education authority average.'

To ensure that 'the central determinant of need is met', and to give schools 'a clear incentive to attract and retain pupils' the total of resources allocated on the basis of numbers of pupils weighted by age (and subject) 'should account for at least 75 per cent of the LEA's total aggregated budget'.

Other factors which local authorities feel they must take into account in drawing up a formula include the social and educational variables which relate to poverty, family structure, linguistic and ethnic mix, and special needs.

Circular 7/88 was eloquently brief about social factors. Coopers and Lybrand noted the practical and theoretical difficulties implicit in preparing an index of social and economic deprivation. The link between such deprivation and a school's need for extra resources is one of judgment, not mathematics. A strong statistical association can be shown between deprivation and poor school performance, but this is not the same thing as causal proof. Various social indicators can be recruited to serve as surrogates for whatever are the actual negative influences, but surrogates are what they are: when it comes to turning these into pounds and pence or staffing schedules, you enter the realm of faith, hope and temperament rather than definitive research.

The Inner London Education Authority was the local education authority which had done most work in this area. It had its own deprivation formula, worked out for its 'Alternative Use of Resources Scheme'. Ironically the Act killed off the ILEA (see Chapter 7) and threatened to break up its research department. To be useful, an index of this kind must be based on up-to-date information – census figures are unlikely to be good enough – and, given the effective abolition of catchment areas by open enrolment, it is necessary to consider the socio-economic characteristics of a school's *actual* pupil population, not just its location and environment.

Inner London recalculated its 'index of educational priority' every two years on the basis of information collected from all primary and secondary schools relating to all their first year entrants and a sample of second, third and fourth year pupils. The factors taken into account have included eligibility for free meals; family size; one-parent families; children in care or fostered; occupation of parents; language other than English (and level of fluency in English); ethnic background; and behaviour (disturbed or not disturbed). (The change in the rules for the provision of school meals in April 1988 removed one widely used social indicator.)

These factors were combined into a score for each school which was then used to weight the distribution of an enlarged capitation allowance placed under the control of the school. The scores were subsequently matched against performance (as measured by examination results) and the weighting refined in the light of experience.

Not many local authorities have the professional expertise at their disposal to set up and maintain an index of this degree of sophistication. Many would have to employ outside consultants should they decide to follow this road.

Coopers and Lybrand envisaged two other elements in the formula, alongside this weighted calculation based on numbers. These were: 'a pragmatic allocation based primarily on the characteristics of the school's site', and what was described as 'limited specific allowances to reflect particular activities at each school'.

The first refers to the intractable questions which are bound to arise about heating, lighting, repairs and maintenance, and how these budget items are to be split up among schools which are of

various ages and in varying states of modernisation and dis-
repair. This has been made all the more serious by the long-term
neglect of school buildings as a result of penny-pinching over the
years. Such neglected maintenance has been signalled in nu-
merous reports by Her Majesty's Inspectors of Schools and by
the DES's own architects. There is no reason to expect that the
Education Reform Act will, of itself, make more funds available
under this head. Any formula is likely to provide schools with a
still inadequate repairs and maintenance budget, while at the
same time giving governors a heightened awareness of the
demands of good stewardship.

In terms of formula-building this sounds like a difficult task. In
terms of politics, it sounds like a convenient way of shifting
responsibility and increasing the pressure on heads and governors to raise their own funds and volunteer labour to carry out
work programmes beyond the limits of the formula.

The 'local school management' complications of community
education and the multiple use of school premises for adult and
youth purposes are more easily recognised than overcome. It is
certainly no part of the stated aims of the Act to discourage the
trend towards closer interaction between schools and their local
communities which has arisen out of a concern that the schools
should be more responsive to the needs of parents and others.
Community education could be said to run in parallel with many
of the Act's underlying ideas. But intentionally or not, the Act
may have made it harder for new community schools to come
into existence and for existing ones to thrive.

School leadership
Local management of schools will only succeed, according to the
Coopers and Lybrand report, 'if there is a positive attitude to it
from the head, the staff and the governing body'. Schools will
only develop such a positive attitude if they conclude that the
benefits outweigh the additional work involved, and if the extra
responsibility is suitably shared. The matter of administrative
help is going to remain high on the agenda. There is an obvious
risk that if sufficient extra clerical and professional assistance is
not forthcoming, financial delegation will take up an increasing
amount of the time of senior teaching staff. In the pilot projects,

already referred to, there was a familiar pattern in secondary schools in which one of the deputy heads came to find bursarial tasks occupying an increasing proportion of his or her time.

Some of the pilot projects have led to suggestions that the office work imposed by local school management can be put at between five and fifteen hours a week. There must be reason to doubt if these estimates adequately reflect the work load which would be generated by a fully operative scheme of delegation. Certainly the picture of managerial activity outlined by the consultants suggests a lot more work for the head's office. If heads and their senior staff are in truth to act like managers of a sizable business, they will have to have assistance on a scale to match the size of the enterprise. A large secondary school can turn over annual sums of the order of £2 million. A business of similar size would expect considerably more administrative back-up than schools have ever received in the past.

The management consultants speak of a 'change in role for staff, headteachers and governors', by which they mean a shift from administering programmes which have been centrally determined elsewhere, to managing a programme controlled by themselves. There has been a great temptation for those who have to promote the message of local school management to exaggerate the impotence of schools under local authority administration while at the same time over-stating the amount of autonomy which the Education Reform Act has promised. Financial delegation will take place within fairly tight financial and educational constraints. Experience suggests the scope for redirection of spending, initially at least, is modest – of the order of two or three per cent.

What this new regime does is force schools to look at their efforts in a new light. They have to discuss and evaluate, and then decide upon, the range of proposals which senior staff bring forward. From this exercise they have to prepare budgets and operating plans. As the consultants point out, they may, in the end, elect to continue as they were before; but if so, it must be by conscious choice and not simply because that is the way it was.

All this suggests a great deal of work for senior staff, competing with all the other tasks imposed by recent reform and innovations, including the national curriculum and new secondary school examinations. The novel element is the linking, at the school itself, of discussions about curriculum and school organisation with budgeting. To make sense of their options, schools need to know a great deal more about themselves – about where resources are presently deployed, and the relative costs of a range of educational options.

Every educational choice entails a choice about the way resources are used – how much teacher time is required, what books and equipment, how many square feet of space. The development of school leadership depends on increasing the flow of the right *kind* of management information: the subtle blend of educational analysis and management accounts which would enable choices to be properly costed, both financially and educationally.

Staffing

The financial sections of the Act are linked to those which deal with staffing. The powers of governing bodies over staff appointments, which were increased in the 1986 Education Act, were further extended in the Education Reform Act. It is the governors who decide whom to employ as teachers and as ancillary staff having due regard to the advice of the chief education officer on the most senior appointments, and on other teaching appointments if they choose to ask for it. It is for the governors to 'manage' the teaching and other staff – that is, be responsible for their appointment, and if necessary their dismissal, and for the distribution of incentive allowances within the limits laid down. The Act makes specific provision for cases of premature retirement, voluntary and involuntary, which seem aimed at encouraging governors to take hold of nettles hitherto allowed to flourish ungrasped.

There are obvious difficulties in transferring all the personnel management responsibilities to the governors, while insisting (as the Act does) that the local education authority remains the employer. These difficulties give rise to the controversial section of the Act (Section 139), which empowers the Secretary of State to make such Orders as he considers necessary to modify the impact of 'any enactment relating to employment' as may be 'necessary or expedient' in regard to the employment of teachers.

The split between employment and management highlights the difficulties which are likely to arise in regard to the relocation of surplus teachers, something for which local authorities have been responsible in the past. Usually relocation has been achieved by persuasion, backed up by a residual authority which could be exercised in the last resort. Relocation is now only possible with the cooperation and agreement of the governors, who can insist on filling posts with their own candidates by national advertisement.

Supply cover remains an important service which local education authorities can offer their schools (where supply staff is available) and this must be expected to continue for some time, at least; otherwise schools would have to make their own arrangements and set aside funds for the purpose.

Role of the local authority

Financial delegation should (ideally) free the local education authority from detailed oversight of most school matters and enable elected members, advised by their senior administrators, to take their larger responsibilities more seriously. These include 'setting objectives for schools' and 'managing the school system as a whole'. Phrases like this, drawn from the consultants' report, are charged with rhetoric and have to be read alongside the curbs on local education initiatives implied by the national curriculum and the limitations on local financial discretion implicit in the reform of local government finance.

Local authorities retain their responsibility for ensuring there are schools for all-comers and they must determine the overall level of spending. They also have to devise the formula and, as we have seen, establish the priorities which it is designed to incorporate.

After the introduction of financial delegation, the most important day-to-day role of the local education authority is to monitor schools' performance and initiate remedial action – or in extreme cases, sanctions – in the case of schools which fail to come up to standard.

To fulfil this task, the local authorities will need expert staff – with a mixture of administrative and pedagogic skills. In former times, the advisory services would have combined many of these professional requirements. In future inspection and advice are to be separated. Inspection is now to be reorganised–'privatised' under the 1992 Education (Schools) Act. Advice and support can come from a variety of sources, public and private. The authority's primary function is judgemental and monitorial. Advice, on the other hand, is sought, or not sought, by the school and paid for out of the school's own budget, whether it comes from the staff of the local authority or from private or academic consultants.

More power at the school level means more power to make mistakes and fail. The local authorities are going to be expected to combine the delegation of day-to-day control with effective supervision and evaluation of performance. To carry out this latter task they need sufficient resources retained under their own control to mount rescue operations in schools which are falling down on the job.

This must include the possibility of sending in trouble-shooters to schools which have got into difficulty. There will be an obvious need to help schools which have begun to lose their popularity with parents, and which are in danger of seeing their school rolls eroded by a process of attrition unless vigorous measures are taken to raise standards and restore the school's reputation.

One element in such monitoring is clearly the testing and assessment built into the national curriculum, and the parental anxieties released when schools are found to be performing badly. Local authorities have to be able to evaluate the information emerging from such measures of performance and, through the professional activities of their own advisers, make their own judgements about the real quality of what schools are doing and how far they are providing value for money.

Accountability becomes a prime objective. Local education authorities can demand to be satisfied at all points that the money which schools have been allocated, and for which they have been made responsible, is well-spent.

In a notoriously difficult field of endeavour, there remains a great deal of work to be done before reliable school performance indicators come to hand.

By the time the Act was passed, a start had been made. Eight local authorities – Staffordshire, Lancashire, Wigan, Rotherham, Dudley, Cheshire, Enfield and Croydon – had agreed to join in a pilot scheme, trying out a set of performance indicators which had been developed by DES statisticians.

The attempt to devise what amount to forms of assessment which go beyond tests of cognitive development and raise questions about good behaviour and attitudes, involves threading a path through a social minefield. But schools have always been about behaviour and attitudes as well as about knowledge and skills, and if they are to be held fully accountable there have to be measurable indicators of how well or badly they perform in these respects.

Governors are likely to be pressed to suggest the indicators by which they, themselves, are prepared to be judged. This may yield some useful aids to good management, but the underlying difficulties will remain.

The Act itself leaves a lot of room for the government of the day to interpret it as it thinks fit. A government which was hostile to local authorities and wished to minimise the scope for them to take important policy decisions of their own, would make sure that only a small amount of uncommitted money remained under the hand of the local authority. This would keep the authority to a strictly limited role – monitoring performance and holding schools accountable to policy edicts issued by the central government.

A government less eager to restrict local political initiatives might deliberately increase the scope for local in-service training and 'school improvement' programmes and allow authorities to retain an adequate budget for this purpose.

Coopers and Lybrand leant towards the latter view, and this is reflected in the draft Circular. The suggestion was that each local education authority might have its own mini-development fund and invite 'bids' from schools interested in particular curriculum initiatives. Central government programmes like the Grant Related In-Service Training scheme have shown how such a device can give local initiative its head, while at the same time chanelling development along pre-stated policy lines. But as Ministerial policy evolved it seemed less and less likely that such local authority initiative would be forthcoming.

Instead there was a hardening of Government attitudes. Ministers were determined that authorities should be required to distribute as much of their budgets to the schools as possible and there were strong attacks on those authorities which 'held back' what Ministers thought were excessive sums for spending at the authority's discretion. There was some irony in these attacks because every one of the English local authorities which had introduced Local Management schemes had done so on terms expressly approved by Ministers.

At this point, a new term of art came into use – the 'Potential Schools Budget' (PSB) – that is, the maximum share of total expenditure which could be distributed to schools after deducting those items which are excluded under Section 38 of the Act. Circular 7/91 laid down that from April, 1993, control of 85 per cent of an authority's PSB must be delegated to schools. Also by April, 1993, 80 per cent of delegated funds must be distributed according to a formula which directly links the money to pupil numbers, weighted for age and special needs. Local Management will be extended to all primary schools by 1994, and by that year, authorities must have in place formulae to enable special schools to exercise delegated powers.

4

Grant-Maintained Schools

Sections 52 to 104

No provision in the Act aroused stronger feelings than those on grant-maintained schools. The aim was to break the local authorities' monopoly of 'maintained' schooling – the provision of free schools, paid for out of public funds. The method chosen was to create a new category of free schools, to be known as 'Grant-Maintained', financed directly by the central government. More than fifty sections were required to achieve this, relatively simple, aim because most of the provisions in other legislation relevant to primary and secondary education had to be adapted and applied to this new class of schools.

Duty to maintain

Section 52 provides the legal basis for a new category of schools financed directly by the Department of Education and Science. It imposes on the Secretary of State a 'duty to maintain' schools set up under the rules laid down in subsequent sections. For primary schools, a minimum of 300 pupils is necessary for a school to be eligible for the new status. The minimum can be changed or abolished by order of the Secretary of State at a future date. All secondary schools are eligible.

Duty of Secretary of State to maintain certain schools
52.—(1) Subject to the provisions of this Chapter ... it shall be the duty of the Secretary of State to maintain any school conducted by a governing body incorporated under this Chapter for the purpose of conducting the school ...

(3) A school to which the Secretary of State's duty under this section for the time being applies shall be known as a grant-maintained school.

Government, powers and conduct

Section 53 concerns the governing body of a grant-maintained school, which must operate under an Instrument of Government made by order of the Secretary of State. Section 53(4) prescribes the composition of the board of governors:

- five elected parents
- not less than one, nor more than two elected teachers
- the head (ex-officio)
- plus a number of 'first' governors ('foundation' governors in the case of an ex-voluntary school) sufficient to form a majority of the whole governing body – i.e. more than the combined total of the elected parents, teachers and head. Two of the 'first' or 'foundation' governors must be current parents.

The names of the members of the initial governing body must be included in the proposal for grant-maintained status (Section 66). In the case of elected members – e.g. parents – elections are to be held if necessary to secure a full complement (sub-sections 2 to 5). The 'existing governing body' – that is, the governing body of the school when it was still a county school – nominates the 'first' governors. In the case of a voluntary school which becomes grant-maintained, the 'foundation' governors are nominated by those who were authorised to nominate foundation governors to the school when it was a voluntary school maintained by a local authority (subsections 7 and 8).

There is also provision for the Secretary of State to make two appointments of his own to the governing body if he thinks that responsibilities are being neglected (Section 53(5)).

After detailing procedural arrangements for the operation of the governing body, the Act goes on (Section 56) to deal with governors' tenure of office: four years for elected governors (parents and teachers) and five to seven years for first or foundation governors.

The governing body of a school which has acquired grant-maintained status is only empowered to conduct a school 'of the same description' as the one which was formerly maintained by the local authority (Section 51(1)). For instance, if it was a comprehensive school when maintained by the local authority, it can only become a grant-maintained comprehensive school; it cannot at the governors' discretion change into, say, a grammar school. Similarly the arrangements for religious education must continue as before.

Having made this stipulation, Section 57 invests the governors of a grant-maintained school with 'the power to do anything which appears to them to be necessary or expedient for the purpose of, or in connection with, the conduct of the school, . . . 'This includes dealing with the premises and land, staffing and finance, including the acceptance of gifts. Grant-maintained schools, like all maintained schools, are debarred from charging fees for admission (Section 106)

In detailing the points to be covered by the Instrument of Government – i.e. the constitution of the governing body, which the Secretary of State must set out by Order – Section 57 goes on to detail the powers the governors are to be given in regard to the holding and acquisition of property and the making of contracts with staff and suppliers.

A grant-maintained school's Articles of Government – i.e. the document which sets out the governors' responsibilities – must also be made by order of the Secretary of State. Section 58 makes provision for this. The articles must comply with any trust deed relating to the school (subsection 3). They must define, in regard to the school, the separate functions of the Secretary of State, the governing body, any committee set up by the governors, and 'any other persons specified . . . in the articles' (subsection 5(a)). The school's admissions arrangements and policy must be set out (subsection 5(b). The document must cover appeals proceedures for parents who contest decisions on admissions and on the expulsion of pupils (subsection 5(d)). (These may be joint procedures with other grant-maintained schools.) The Articles must provide for parental appeals on curriculum matters. Provisions have to be made to cover staff discipline (subsections 5(g) and (h) and to apply to grant-maintained schools general requirements for the publication of an annual report, the holding of an annual parents' meeting and the duty to have regard to the views of the local police chief or other community representatives on the secular curriculum.

Procedure for acquisition of grant-maintained status

Section 60 lays down the rules which must apply when a local authority maintained school – county or voluntary – seeks to become grant-maintained.

The decision to apply rests with the parents, in a secret postal ballot. Such a ballot can be called in two ways.

The governors can insist on a ballot by a simple majority vote at two meetings, held not less than 28 days or more than 42 days apart.

A ballot can also be requisitioned by a written demand signed by 'a number of parents of registered pupils at the school equal to at least 20 per cent of the number of registered pupils at the school'.

It is left to the governors to decide in case of doubt who is to be accepted as a parent of a registered pupil (Section 60(10)), having regard to guidance issued by the DES. The governors must organise the ballot within three months of receiving a valid request from sufficient parents, or passing a second resolution themselves. If they vote to hold a ballot they must tell the local authority, and in the case of a voluntary school, the Trustees (who in the case of a Roman Catholic school will normally be representatives of the diocesan bishop.)

Procedure for acquisition of grant-maintained status
60.—(1) In the case of any school which is eligible for grant-maintained status, a ballot of parents on the question of whether grant-maintained status should be sought for the school shall be held in accordance with section 61 of this Act if either—

    (a) the governing body decide by a resolution passed at a meeting of that body ("the first resolution") to hold such a ballot and confirm that decision ... by a resolution ("the second resolution") passed at a subsequent meeting of the governing body held not less than twenty-eight days, nor more than forty-two days, after that at which the first resolution was passed; or

    (b) they receive a written request to hold such a ballot which meets the requirements of subsection (2) below.

(2) Those requirements are that the request must be signed (or otherwise endorsed in such manner as the governing body may require) by a number of parents of registered pupils at the school equal to at least twenty per cent of the number of registered pupils at the school on the date on which the request is received....

Section 61 lays down in detail how the 'secret postal ballot' is to be conducted. Governors must also heed additional guidance given by the Secretary of State. They must tell all parents about the poll and explain the procedure for casting a vote. They must provide information about the proposed change of status, the constitution of the proposed new governing body and a 'general explanation' of how the school is to be funded and conducted. Voters must be given the names and addresses of the initial governing body. Section 61(12) gives the Secretary of State the power to reimburse the governors for the costs of the ballot.

If on the day appointed for the ballot more than half of those eligible to vote do take part, the issue of whether to go ahead with the opting-out proposal is decided by a simple majority vote.

If, on the other hand, less than half of those eligible to take part actually cast their votes, then the result is set aside and a second ballot must be held within 14 days. This second vote then decides the issue by a simple majority.

> **61.**—(8) Where in the case of any ballot held in respect of a school in accordance with this section other than one held by virtue of this subsection ("the first ballot") the total number of votes cast in the ballot by persons eligible to vote in the ballot is less than fifty per cent of the number of persons so eligible, it shall be the duty of the governing body to secure that another ballot ("the second ballot") is held before the end of the period of fourteen days beginning with the date immediately following that on which the result of the first ballot is determined.

If the parents vote in favour of opting out, the governors then have six months in which to publish detailed proposals for the acquisition of grant-maintained status, forwarding a copy to the Secretary of State.

Section 62 sets out the information which they must supply. The proposals must state the result of the ballot, with the voting figures. They must describe the school, its character and status, and provide such other information as the Secretary of State may prescribe.

> **62.**—(1) This section applies where in the case of any school which is eligible for grant-maintained status the result of a ballot held in accordance with section 61 of this Act shows a simple majority of votes cast in the ballot by persons eligible to vote in the ballot (within the meaning of that section) in favour of seeking grant-maintained status for the school.
>
> (2) It shall be the duty of the governing body of the school, before the end of the period of six months beginning with the date on which the result of the ballot is determined, to—
>
> > (a) publish proposals for acquisition of grant-maintained status for the school . . .
> >
> > (b) submit to the Secretary of State a copy of the published proposals.

The statement must include details of the arrangements which the school intends to make for the admission of pupils, the provision for pupils with special educational needs, the induction of newly qualified teachers, and the in-service training and professional development of all the members of the teaching staff.

As well as setting out how the school is to be run under new management, and the names and addresses of the members of the governing body, the proposals must include a notice giving objectors two months in which to send their observations to the Secretary of State.

Objections can be submitted by:

- ten or more local electors
- the Trustees (if any)
- the governing bodies of any other schools affected by the proposals
- any local authority concerned.

Then it is up to the Secretary of State to consider the proposals and the objections, and, having done so, to accept or reject or modify them as he thinks fit. If he approves, the new governing body takes over and the change of status goes ahead.

Section 64 repeats many of the provisions of Section 53 in detailing the arrangements for the 'initial' governing bodies which take over on the grant of new status. Subsequent sections (65–72, together with Schedule 5) deal with transitional arrangements between the former governing body and the initial governors.

Proposals for closure or changes in schools eligible for grant-maintained status

Special consideration is given in Section 73 to the possibility that a school might seek grant-maintained status at the same time as the local authority is trying to close it or alter its character.

If an opting-out proposal is in the pipeline, the local authority must postpone any plan for closure or alteration till the Secretary of State has decided whether the school in question may be allowed to go grant-maintained. If a closure proposal and an opting-out application are on the table at the same time, the Secretary of State must consider the two together, but must decide on the opting-out question before accepting or rejecting the local authority's closure or alteration scheme.

Property and staff

Other sections cover the transfer of property and staff to a grant-maintained school. Staff contracts are transferred by Section 75(7) and (8) to the new employer (the governors of the grant-maintained school). Similarly, the grant-maintained school acquires any property rights and liabilities inherited from the school's former existence.

Finance

Arrangements for the payment of grants to grant-maintained schools are detailed in Section 79. The grants include maintenance grants for running costs. Others can be made for capital expenditure; for specific purposes decided by the Secretary of State (in parallel, for example, with specific grants made to the local authority sector); for in-service training, and for special programmes like those in connection with the urban programme.

The local education authorities are to be no better off or worse off financially as a result of a school becoming grant-maintained. Sections 81 and 82 lay down the rules which allow the Secretary of State to recoup from the local authority, in respect of an opted-out school, what would have been spent maintaining the school had it not changed status.

Under the Act's local financial delegation clauses (see Chapter 3), local authorities have to establish a formula for the distribution of most of the education budget to schools, holding back only certain items like loan charges, central administration and some support services. This calculation will serve as the basis for establishing the budget for a grant-maintained school.

Admissions
Grant-maintained schools are required, like county schools, to admit pupils up to their 'standard number' (Section 83).

Change of character
It has already been stated that a local authority school which acquires grant-maintained status must retain its previous 'character'. Section 89 provides a mechanism (similar to that in sections 12 and 13 of the 1980 Act) for the publication of notices and the hearing of objections after which it is for the Secretary of State to consider whether to approve, reject or modify a 'significant change of character' or significant enlargement of the premises of a grant-maintained school. No such proposal may go forward from an ex-voluntary school without the agreement of the Trustees.

Religious worship and education
Sections 84 to 88 keep grant-maintained schools in line with local authority maintained schools in regard to the daily act of worship and the provision of religious education, with the appropriate rights of withdrawal for parents who do not wish their children to attend.

This means that in all ex-county schools, and for most children in ex-voluntary Controlled schools, religious education will be in accordance with the Agreed Syllabus (Sections 84–85), while in ex-Aided schools, the provisions of the Trust Deed will normally apply (Section 86).

The act of worship in an ex-county school must be 'wholly or broadly of a mainly Christian character' without being distinctive of any particular Christian denomination. There are provisions for flexibility in the interpretation of this rule: every act of worship does not need to be Christian in character so long as 'taking any school term as a whole' the school meets the requirement. There is no provision for an application to the local Standing Advisory Council on Religious Education for an exemption from the requirement for Christian worship.

To alter these arrangements, the provisions for a 'change of character' would have to be invoked.

Discontinuance

Grant-maintained schools can only be discontinued under rules laid down in Section 92. If governors want to discontinue, they have to submit proposals to the Secretary of State. Before he decides what to do he must consider objections from the public, from other governing bodies, and from the local education authorities.

Section 93 deals with cases where it is the Secretary of State who initiates a move to withdraw grant-maintained status. He can do this at any time, giving seven years' notice. In the case of mismanagement, he has power under Section 53(5) to appoint two extra governors of his own choosing. If the mismanagement continues, or if numbers fall below a viable level, he can, after due warnings have been given, cease to maintain the school from a date determined by him.

Procedures for winding up a school and its property are set out in Section 94. The Act also envisages circumstances in which, on ceasing to be grant-maintained, a school re-emerges with a different status – say independent or voluntary aided – and deals with the questions of capital value which arise.

Grant-maintained schools are entitled to continue to receive certain services from the local education authority after having opted out. Section 100 puts a duty on the local authority not to treat the grant-maintained schools and their pupils any less favourably than its own schools. These services include making payments for board and lodging, providing home-to-school transport, and providing clothing for pupils.

Background

Such was the hostility which the grant-maintained school proposal aroused among all sections of the educational establishment that it was difficult, as the Bill went through Parliament, to get the issues it raised discussed dispassionately and accurately.

Powerful vested interests were at work. The local education authorities saw the whole matter in terms of the 'loss' of schools from 'our' sector, and thought of opting out as a form of treachery or defection.

The Department of Education and Science, on the other hand, saw it as the opportunity at last to get executive authority over a whole category of schools. Having for many years been obliged to act indirectly through the local education authorities, the Department was now offered a new and enlarged responsibility and greatly welcomed the change of role.

As for opinion among teachers, this reflected an underlying suspicion that what was intended was the break-up of the existing maintained school system with a view to more radical change at a later stage – privatisation, say, or the reintroduction of a selective system of grammar schools and secondary moderns. The teachers' unions sided with the local authorities – their employers – with many of whom they shared a belief in comprehensive secondary education and a hostility to the creation of another category of schools which might be expected to institutionalise, in a new and (as they saw it) dangerous way, an invidious pecking order among schools.

The fires of political controversy were fanned by the reasons given for creating this new class of school. It was held to be necessary to provide alternatives for parents in areas where political extremists had gained control over the local education authority. It was envisaged, for example, that parents in deprived areas, where public services (including education) were at their least effective, might vote their schools out of local authority control and into grant-maintained status.

In presenting the new type of school as a way of escape for schools in boroughs dominated by their political opponents, the sponsors of the new Act injected a polemic note into the discussion from the outset. The new type of school was to be seen as a means by which parents could place the education of their children beyond the reach of the local education authority and its policy on, say, comprehensive education or racism or gender issues.

It was assumed that this mechanism would be of particular interest to surviving grammar schools in areas threatening to go comprehensive, or seeking to complete comprehensive schemes already begun.

It was also possible to foresee schools trying to evade the consequences of reorganisation schemes by opting out rather than face closure or the loss of a sixth form. The Act made provision for such possibilities in Section 89 which, as we have seen, lays down how the Secretary of State should deal with proposals for grant-maintained status which coincide with local authority reorganisation schemes: the opting out proposal must be disposed of first, but only after the Secretary of State has considered it and the reorganisation scheme side by side.

Governing bodies

The Act placed great weight on the need for would-be grant-maintained schools to attract a competent set of 'first' or 'foundation' governors. There was even a clause (53(9)) which described the type of citizen schools should look for:

> 'the kind of person who may be appointed as a first governor of a grant-maintained school is a person appearing to the persons appointing him to be a member of the local community who is committed to the good government and continuing viability of the school'.

At least two of the first governors must be parents of children currently attending the school. There is the further provision that the first governors must include 'members of the local business community'.

Great importance must attach to the ability and standing of proposed chairpersons for such governing bodies, on whom much of the responsibility inevitably devolves. The job of the chairperson is always going to depend on how much administrative help is available. The Act is not concerned with whether grant-maintained schools have full-time bursars or how the clerking of the governors' meetings is to be dealt with. But it does make clear that governors will have to take responsibility for the school as a working institution and for all the commercial transactions it engages in.

The ballot

The Act makes various provisions for the balloting of parents on whether to apply for grant-maintained status. These aroused considerable discussion during the passage of the Bill and have wide implications for its implementation.

First, there was the matter of the franchise for such a ballot. The Act makes the school governors responsible for deciding who is or is not eligible to vote' but in a litigious age, governors will have to act with care and pay close attention to the guidelines issued by the DES.

Parents do not have a vote in respect of more than one child at any single school. But who is a parent? The question was already important in regard to elections for parent-governors, but the all-or-nothing significance of an opt-out vote meant that rough and ready decisions by harassed heads were now much more likely to be challenged.

As well as natural parents living together, parents may include step-parents, unmarried partners of natural parents, and other permutations of formal and informal family relationships. Some children may have more than two 'parents' for the purpose of balloting. Others, including children in local authority care, have guardians who may or may not be eligible to vote. Children from broken families may carry more votes than those of single parents or 'Janet and John' families.

Governors are obliged (Section 61(3)) to 'take . . . such steps as are reasonably practical to secure that every person who is eligible to vote 'is given details of the proposals for opting out and how to vote. In practice the task of compiling the register of parents falls on heads. 'Reasonably practical' means what it says. Governors have to make every reasonable effort to assemble an electoral list but will not be held responsible if some absent 'parents' slip through the net.

The DES confirmed this reading by issuing an Administrative Memorandum (1/88) which amends the Pupils' Registration Regulations (1956) on the keeping of school records. This points out that 'parent' in this context does not necessarily mean natural parent: 'it could include step parents or an adult who is effectively responsible for the welfare of the child but is not a blood relation'. Recognising the trouble which intrusive inquiries might cause, the DES advises that heads should take reasonable steps to identify parents, but that exhaustive investigation is not expected if parents choose not to offer information.

There will, however, be considerable difficulty, particularly in areas with ethnic minority populations and complex patterns of family life which may or may not correspond to the expectations of governors and pressure groups. It also suggests that pressure groups will find plenty of scope for identifying potential voters who have been missed off lists, with a corresponding risk of electoral fraud and disputation by dissatisfied individuals and organisations. Section 61(11) gives the Secretary of State wide powers to declare a ballot void and require a fresh one to be held.

Second, there was the question of how the ballot should be interpreted. For a ballot to be called, the Bill, as drafted, required the votes of a simple majority of governors or a requisition signed by a number of parents equal to 20 per cent of the number of registered pupils. An amendment was accepted in Committee which required the governors to meet and vote in favour of a ballot twice, at an interval of not less than four weeks, for this to have the legal effect of forcing a parental poll.

The original Bill laid down that an opting-out proposal had to go ahead if it was backed by a simple majority of parents voting in a single ballot. This aroused strong opposition from a wide range of critics in the local authorities, teachers' unions, churches, parents' organisations and others. In Committee, Dr Keith Hampson, the Conservative member for Leeds North West, attempted to muster Conservative resistance but without success. Opponents of the clause favoured a requirement for a qualified majority – more than 50 per cent of the parents eligible to vote – or at least provision for a minimum poll. The Government successfully fended off Dr Hampson, arguing that many electoral decisions had to be taken on the basis of a vote by those interested enough to exercise their franchise. MPs themselves (not to mention local councillors) received their mandate in this way. They rejected the precedents of the referendum on Scottish devolution (where a qualified majority had been insisted on) and trade union legislation which requires 85 per cent of those voting to justify a closed shop. The argument was never seriously joined on issues of principle because the practical politics of the matter were plain: the supporters of a qualified majority disliked opting out and wanted to make it more difficult. The Government favoured opting out and wanted to place no additional obstruction in its way.

In the House of Lords, the Bishop of London took up the case argued earlier by Dr Hampson and persuaded the Upper House to vote for an amendment which made opting out conditional on a vote by an absolute majority of parents. The Government refused to accept this and when the Bill returned to the House of Commons the simple majority was reinstated, but with the proviso that if, in a first ballot, less than 50 per cent of the eligible voters take part, a second ballot should be held two weeks later. A simple majority in the second ballot would then be binding.

Under the revised arrangements it will still be possible for a minority of parents to vote a school out of the local authority system. But only after two ballots have been held and there has been every attempt to publicise the issues and get parents to the poll. There must be a risk that the second poll will be thinner than the first – even that a proposal which is rejected on a small poll at the first ballot will be approved at a second ballot on an even smaller one. But the final decision will, in any case, rest with the Secretary of State (another example of his large powers under the Act). It will be for him to assess the evidence which the ballot provides – how far it suggests strong parental support – alongside the other material which the proposers produce to support their scheme. In the debate on the Bill, Mr Kenneth Baker emphasised that he would not approve a scheme unless he was sure it had solid support among the parents. A thin poll would deter any minister from pressing forward.

The hundredth grant maintained school – the Arnewood school in Hampshire – was approved in July, 1991. Some fifty more schools had begun the opting out procedure. Applications had come forward at a quickening pace in 1990–91, strongly encouraged by Mr Kenneth Clarke. Restrictions on the granting of grant maintained status to primary schools were lifted – the first three were allowed to opt out in the summer of 1991.

As expected, one of the most common reasons for opting-out appeared to be to avoid closure or merger under a local authority reorganisation scheme. Local authorities argued that this would discourage plans for taking surplus places out of service in future. Ministers resolutely refused to accept this, pointing to a slow, but steady flow of reorganisation schemes which authorities were bringing forward. Nevertheless, it seems fairly clear that in some counties and cities, reorganisation plans were shelved while authorities strove to fend off threats of opting-out.

Staff

The staff of a county or voluntary school which opts out, transfer en bloc to the grant-maintained school, with pay and conditions of service equivalent to those enjoyed before the change of status. Anyone who objects has, of course, the option of resigning. Section 75(8) makes it clear that someone who decides to go simply because of an objection to the change of employer cannot claim redundancy. Governors, thereafter, have responsibility for appointments and for staffing levels, and the discretion to decide how to distribute incentive allowances. It will also be for the governors to deal with suspensions and dismissals (subject to the terms of the Instrument of Government) and questions arising from early retirement, voluntary or involuntary. The consultative paper issued while the Bill was in preparation suggested that special grants might be available to pay for dismissals and premature retirements during the first twelve months of the life of a grant-maintained school.

The Government was anxious to ensure that grant-maintained school governors had more discretion over whom they could appoint as teachers than the governors of county and voluntary schools – for example, by not insisting on formal 'teacher training' by way of a post-graduate certificate of education or a B.Ed. degree. Teachers appointed to grant-maintained schools are not subject to the probation arrangements which apply to teachers at county and voluntary schools. For this reason, opting-out proposals have to include details of how the governors propose to arrange for the induction of new teachers.

Finance

How well off are grant-maintained schools? The formal answer is that they are to treated no more, no less generously than the schools in their locality. Because they do not receive support services from the local authority, except by special arrangement (and payment), their grant from the DES is bigger than the money put at the disposal of neighbouring county schools under the financial delegation proposals (see Chapter 3). But out of this margin they have to finance their own administration, and provide in their own budgets for support services such as psychological consultancy and in-service training.

This is clearly what the Act implies and what ministers said it meant when it was being debated, but the Act itself only sets out a legal method of ensuring that a local authority is neither better nor worse off if one of its schools opts out. Grant regulations governing the relation between the DES and grant-maintained schools came into operation in September 1989 – only days before the first such schools opened – and a Circular (21/89) gave general guidance.

Special provisions apply to the transitional stage during which a school is completing the formalities between the approval of proposals and the incorporation of the school under its new governing body and constitution.

The Secretary of State has considerable discretion over the provision of grants for opted-out schools, including 100 per cent capital grants, and grants for specific purposes. These include grants to cover a grant-maintained school's increased liability for VAT. The Secretary of State may provide funds to cover the cost of 'staff restructuring during the first year', and certain costs associated with the school premises and insurance. These are met by additional funds from the Exchequer and are not recovered from the local education authority.

Grant-maintained schools also receive money from the DES to replace funds which might otherwise be received under the Local Government Act of 1966 in respect of ethnic minority students; under the TVEI scheme; under the local education authority training grants; and under the Education Support Grants made by the DES under approved programmes. In the case of these payments, there is a corresponding reduction in central grants to local authorities, to maintain the principle of financial neutrality. The grant-maintained schools in any area will receive a sum equivalent to the average spending by their local authority per primary and secondary school under each of these programmes.

It was clear from the start that if grant-maintained status did not prove attractive on the terms first propounded, the Secretary of State had ample discretion within the relevant Sections of the Act to increase the financial incentives.

As it happened, applications were slow in coming in during the first two years, but Ministers showed they were determined to make opting out worth while. They used their powers to give grant-maintained schools generous capital grants. Transitional grants were increased to provide an instant and undisguised encouragement. A secondary school which opts out may well receive an immediate six figure increase in its annual budget. And the procedure for calculating annual maintenance grants from the DES – the main element in a grant-maintained school's income – was simplified.

This was still to be related to the budgetary provisions of the local authority which formerly maintained the school, but instead of haggling over the exact amount withheld by the authority for centrally-funded services, grant-maintained schools everywhere were to be credited with a standard 16 per cent (later reduced to 15 per cent). The result of the change was marginally favourable to the grant maintained schools over all; more particularly, it helped by giving them much earlier financial information on which to base their plans.

The retention of the link between the level of funding for grant-maintained schools and that which applies to other county and voluntary schools in their immediate area, ensures that the resources of grant-maintained schools, like those of county schools, will vary to a marked degree from one part of the country to another. A grant-maintained school in Inner London, for instance, could expect to receive an annual grant which was twice as much as a school which opted out in – say – Hereford and Worcester. How long this will remain tolerable is an open question. Grant-maintained schools will certainly highlight the anomalies which lie behind these gross discrepancies. Acting together through the organisations which come into existence to represent them, they are likely to generate a powerful lobby.

The embryo of such an organisation was formed in the summer of 1988. The Grant Maintained Schools Trust was set up, with Mr Steve Norris as chairman (Mr Norris became Conservative MP for Epping at a bye-election in December 1988), to offer help and encouragement to schools considering whether to aim at opting out. By the time the Act reached the Statute Book, the Trust's director, Mr Andrew Turner, claimed to be in touch with up to 150 schools. In its first phase the Trust exists to promote the idea of grant-maintained schools and persuade potential applicants to go ahead. But as the movement gathers pace, its character is bound to change and instead of being primarily a promotional body it may well become a representative pressure group on behalf of the grant-maintained schools.

One of the early objects of such a lobby might well be to break the link between the funding of grant-maintained schools and the funding of local authority schools in the area in which they happen to be situated.

It is not obvious that this would necessarily run counter to the instincts of some future Secretary of State, although averaging out the level of funding for opted-out schools would inevitably have the unpopular consequence of taking away resources from half of them. The method of financing chosen was the only realistic one open to the authors of the Act if it was a condition precedent that the change should be made without adding to the total cost. But it does mean that schools in low cost areas have to weigh carefully the immediate benefits which they stand to receive as a result of the 'bribes' offered to encourage opting out, against the fact that they would thereafter have to make ends meet without having County Hall at their back in times of trouble.

Even schools which opt out in areas of very high spending would have to face the prospect that the strenuous efforts being made to curb such spending will succeed in the end. When this happens, the grant-maintained schools in those areas will lose grant and feel the squeeze along with the county and voluntary schools.

One radical Conservative vision is for grant-maintained status to become the norm, replacing vouchers as the favoured vehicle for market choice in schooling. Such a view was expounded by Mrs Margaret Thatcher when she was Prime Minister. Similar sentiments were expressed in January 1991 by Mr Kenneth Clarke. Mrs Thatcher thought opting out would be as popular as the sale of council houses; Clarke drew an analogy with changes taking place in the National Health Service.

What is clear is that, if the political control of the education service remains unchanged in the mid-1990s, the number of grant-maintained schools will increase rapidly – so rapidly as to put strain on the DES regional administrative arrangements, and to make it impossible to continue to offer special financial incentives to encourage schools to opt out.

Accountability

As direct-grant institutions, receiving their money from the Treasury, grant-maintained schools are subject to the regulations which the Secretary of State makes to ensure that the funds are properly accounted for. This accountability extends beyond rules about book-keeping and audit, to standards of performance and guarantees about the implementation of the national curriculum.

The assumption behind the Act is that opting out will bring freedom and independence to schools formerly controlled by local authorities. How big a difference the change of regime makes will depend on how detailed are the arrangements for monitoring financial and educational performance, and how far the requirements of central bureaucracy impinge on individual schools. The Act gives the Secretary of State responsibility for, and power over, the grant-maintained schools and the assumption must be that he will use it. The grant-maintained schools will be among those institutions which experience the tensions implicit in a policy which is at one and the same time centralist and decentralising in intent.

Change of character

The Act is clear that grant-maintained schools can only change 'character' by going through the procedures laid down in sections 12 and 13 of the 1980 Education Act, which require the publication of notices and the opportunity for objectors to make a case to the Secretary of State before he decides whether to approve, reject or modify the proposal. A local authority maintained school, whether county or voluntary, which acquires grant-maintained status does so within its pre-existing 'character', a term which embraces its size, its academic model (grammar, comprehensive, secondary modern) and its religious basis or ethos.

It is important to note, then, that governors of grant-maintained schools will not be able to decide, unilaterally, on matters which affect the 'character' of the school. Some critics jumped to the conclusion that grant-maintained schools were really a back-door method of reintroducing selective secondary education. In this, they were encouraged perhaps by some misleading answers given by the Prime Minister during the 1987 General Election campaign. Mrs Thatcher suggested that the schools would be able to set selection tests and, also, charge fees. These 'misunderstandings' were cleared up by Mr Kenneth Baker, the Education Secretary, and the Act itself is perfectly clear about the procedure.

Before the Bill was drafted, there had been an assurance from Mr Baker that no proposal for a change of character would be entertained within five years of a school acquiring grant-maintained status. This stipulation did not appear in the Bill itself but was repeated in a DES Circular in October 1988.

By the spring of 1991, the mood had changed again, and the Education Secretary, Mr Kenneth Clarke, withdrew the undertaking, telling a conference of grant-maintained school heads that he saw little 'worthwhile purpose' in the five-year rule. 'I am prepared . . . to consider proposals for change of character put to me by GM schools at any sensible interval after they are established . . . Of those that do opt for change, I anticipate that few schools will seek to introduce selective admissions. But some may well wish to publish proposals for establishing sixth forms or becoming single sex or co-educational. What I am utterly convinced of is that grant-maintained school status for schools in Britain will become the norm. Indeed I *want* GM status to be the norm.' (It can only be assumed that the reference to Britain was a slip of the tongue on the part of the English Secretary of State, not a declaration of imperial intent.)

The admissions procedures for grant-maintained schools are covered by the Articles of Government of each school – meaning that, when he approves a new opted-out school, the Secretary of State includes a section in its constitution dealing with admissions, and with appeals and complaints against decisions of the governing body. Those refused places at grant-maintained schools will not, of course, have access to the local authority's appeals committees.

If a grant-maintained school is popular and heavily over-subscribed, it is for the governors, in the light of the Articles of Government, to decide which pupils to accept and which to reject. This will be no different, in essence, from the situation which might arise in similar circumstances in a Voluntary Aided School. In such cases, it is not unusual for schools to be accused of using their control of admissions to discriminate unfairly against particular groups of pupils – for example, blacks or socially-disadvantaged or simply difficult and disagreeable children. All the Act does is to say it is up to the governors to act in accordance with their Articles of Government and the law of the land, including their obligation to maintain the character of the school unchanged.

The Churches
The Churches, jointly and severally, took an immediate dislike to the proposals for grant-maintained schools. They had worked for many years closely with the local education authorities to make a success of the 1944 Education Act and the settlement of the religious question which it incorporated. Contrary to popular myth, the 1944 settlement was not accepted without demur. The Roman Catholics accepted it under protest. R. A. Butler's achievement in 1943–44, however, was to get it through without any serious disruption to the war effort and without any serious breach in the consensus which supported the Act as a whole.

Under the 1944 Act, there were two categories of 'voluntary' schools which were also 'maintained' – that is, their running costs were paid for by the local education authority. *Aided* schools remained denominationally-directed. Religious instruction was in accordance with the provision of the Trust-Deed – i.e. it could reflect the credal assumptions of the Church – and the Trustees nominated a majority of the governors. Aided schools were responsible for their own curriculum and admissions. *Controlled* schools, on the other hand, had a majority of local authority nominees on their governing bodies, and, with certain minor exceptions, religious instruction had to follow the Agreed Syllabus, as in county schools. Curricula and admissions were a matter for the local authority.

The differences in the degree of church influence were reflected in the financial arrangements set out in 1944. In the case of controlled schools, capital expenditure was met by the local education authority. In the case of Aided schools, the voluntary school authorities – usually the Church of England or the Roman Catholics – had to find 50 per cent of the cost. This was far beyond their means, and progressively, between 1944 and 1975, the size of the Churches' capital contribution was reduced to 15 per cent.

A majority of the Church of England schools became controlled; the Roman Catholics insisted on Aided status for their schools. By 1988 the position in England and Wales was as follows:

Church of England schools			
Aided	*Pupils*	*Controlled*	*Pupils*
2076	378382	2954	411604

Roman Catholic schools	
Aided	*Pupils*
2400	657328

At first sight, it might appear that grant-maintained status had a great deal to offer to the Churches, financially. If all Aided schools were to opt out there would be an immediate end to the obligation to pay 15 per cent of future capital expenditure. And as the 'character' of a grant-maintained ex-Aided school can only be changed after going through the hoops of publishing notices and hearing objections, the Churches could be reasonably assured that they would continue to be in the driving seat.

This was not the view they took. They noted that, under the terms of the Bill, parents could (albeit in fairly unlikely circumstances) vote their school into being a candidate for grant-maintained status against the wishes of the Trustees. They argued strongly for the Trustees to be given a veto but this was resisted throughout the Committee stage in the House of Commons. They did win a minor concession which gave the Trustees a veto on applications for a change of 'character'. But the Government insisted that if the Churches wanted to hold on to their privileges they would have to do so by keeping their own appointed governors in line. About the time the Bill was published, the Cardinal Archbishop of Westminster was having difficulty in doing just this with the governors of a London comprehensive, Cardinal Vaughan School. This involved litigation and adverse publicity.

As Trustee, Cardinal Hume tried to replace governors nominated by him who had gone against his wishes (and the policy of the diocese) in supporting an opt-out proposal. The issue ended in the Court of Appeal which refused to allow the Cardinal to remove the dissidents and replace them with new nominees of his own persuasion. It became necessary for him to appoint governors to the proposed grant-maintained school governing body, which he did with great reluctance, to comply with the law. Compliance meant appointing the kind of governors described in Section 53(9) – members of the local community 'committed to the good government and continuing viability of the school' in its new guise. So the Trustee, though opposed in principle to the change in the school's status, could nevertheless be required to nominate as foundation governors, men or women who were directly opposed to the wishes of the Trustee and the foundation. Another case, concerning the Trinity School at Leamington Spa, also brought governors into dispute with the diocesan authorities.

These cases, taken together with one involving the Inner London Education Authority which had sought to remove ILEA-nominated governors from Haberdasher's Aske's (Hatcham) school for boys, because they had supported a proposal to turn the school into a city technology college, demonstrated the modest nature of the powers of both local authorities and Trustees in controlling the actions of their nominees.

The powers of the Roman Catholic authorities in these matters – though less than satisfactory to them – are greater and more effective than those at the disposal of the Anglicans, whose Trustees are liable to be a law unto themselves.

The Government's refusal to budge on the issue reflected an awareness that Roman Catholic lay people did not wholly share the hierarchy's liking for tight discipline. The Duke of Norfolk, the senior Roman Catholic layman in the House of Lords, brushed the Bishops' objections aside and the Upper House refused to amend the Bill to strengthen the position of the Church authorities.

The Churches' objections to the opting-out proposal went beyond the specific question of whether it would be possible for a church school to become secularised or disobedient to the Bishops. Like the local authorities, they believed that the creation of a new tier of schools, with funding direct from the DES would be divisive. They quite simply did not want the kind of organisation of schools which lay at the root of the Government's thinking. They thought this would set school against school and encourage a damaging rivalry, rather than healthy competition. As has already been mentioned, they regarded their schools as being organised in diocesan 'systems' – interdependent networks in which all had a common interest in the success of each. The Roman Catholic bishops expressed the view most strongly on behalf of their own schools:

> '[Opting out'] favours the interests of a minority of parents and children at the expense of the majority. Such a general principle is difficult to reconcile with Catholic ideals.'

All the Churches, including the Church of England, shared this general view of the damage which opting out might do to the rest of the system – to the county and voluntary Controlled schools, no less than to the Aided.

This attitude could well change when the initial shock of the Education Reform Act wears off. If grant-maintained schools enjoy high prestige, as most people seem to assume they will, the Churches will be forced to come to terms with the fact that they will be popular with their lay people. If there prove to be added financial incentives, over and above the entitlement to 100 per cent capital grants, it will be doubly difficult for the Churches to maintain their opposition. A change of Government would put the grant-maintained schools in immediate jeopardy, but if they survive into the mid-1990s it would not be surprising if they became as generally accepted as the former Direct Grant schools.

If these schools survive the political hazards which attend them, there must be a strong possibility that many will apply for a change of 'character' and seek to re-emerge as selective schools in a new form – not necessarily schools recruiting on strictly academic merit: possibly, like City Technology Colleges, they might rely more heavily on tests of motivation and parental support.

What is clear, once again, is that there is room for considerable development of the grant-maintained school concept, and this development will depend on political movements outside the education system in the country at large.

5

Higher and Further Education

Sections 120 to 138

The sections on higher and further education give effect to the decision to remove advanced further education from the control of local education authorities. The opportunity is taken to clear up doubts about the legal basis of further education by replacing or repealing obsolete sections of the 1944 Education Act. But these sections were themselves repealed by the Higher and Further Education Act, 1992 which removed further education from local authority control and set up a Further Education Funding Council.

For the universities, a new statutory Universities Funding Council is set up in place of the University Grants Committee; and a Polytechnics and Colleges Funding Council takes over responsibility for funding higher education in the polytechnics, the other former local authority colleges, and the voluntary colleges of higher education. The Higher and Further Education Act, 1992 replaced these bodies with a combined Higher and Further Education Funding Council – see also note on page 100.

Local duties and powers

Section 120 distinguishes between higher and further education. Local authorities were given a general duty to provide adequate facilities for further education, and a discretionary power to secure the provision of higher education 'appropriate to the needs of their area'. Higher education is defined by a list of eight types of course leading to degrees, diplomas and professional qualifications set out in Schedule 6 of the Act. These definitions embrace most of the work covered by the Polytechnics and Colleges Funding Council and the Universities Funding Council.

Further education is defined as full- and part-time education and training (other than higher education) for those who have left school and are beyond the compulsory school age, and who may be in or out of employment; and for 'organised leisure-time occupation in connection with the provision of such education and training'.

In their planning for both further and higher education, local authorities are required to 'have regard to' any educational facilities available within their area provided by universities, polytechnics and other colleges of higher education.

Legal basis

This restatement of local authority responsibilities involves replacing sections 41 and 42 of the 1944 Education Act. Section 120(5) sweeps away the 1944 Act requirement for local authorities to prepare 'schemes' for further education subject to approval by the Secretary of State, and repeals the never-implemented provisions relating to County Colleges. New requirements for further education schemes of a different kind come in Section 139 *et seq*.

LOCAL EDUCATION AUTHORITY FUNCTIONS WITH RESPECT TO HIGHER
AND FURTHER EDUCATION

120.—(2) The following section shall be substituted for section 41 of the 1944 Act—

> 41.—(1) It shall be the duty of every local education authority to secure the provision for their area of adequate facilities for further education.
>
> (2) Subject to the following provisions of this section, in this Act "further education" means—
>
>> (a) full-time and part-time education for persons over compulsory school age (including vocational, social, physical and recreational training); and
>>
>> (b) organized leisure-time occupation provided in connection with the provision of such education. . . .

Higher education corporations

Sections 121 to 128 deal with arrangements for the colleges which have become part of the PCFC sector to become 'higher education corporations'.

Section 121(1) requires the Secretary of State to specify which institutions are affected, using criteria for eligibility laid down in Section 121(2). To qualify for corporate status a college has to have a full-time equivalent enrolment of at least 350 on advanced courses, and these full-time advanced students must be at least 55 per cent of the total. A college also is eligible if it has a full-time equivalent enrolment of at least 2500 students for such courses. Section 122 provides for the Secretary of State to add other colleges to the list by Order at a future date if the circumstances of individual colleges justify.

Section 124 sets out what a higher education corporation can do: provide higher education and courses of a less advanced character; carry out research; employ staff; supply goods and services; borrow money; hold property; make investments and enter into joint ventures; and create scholarships. Each college has to have its own constitution, its Articles of Government, approved by the Secretary of State (Section 125).

These Articles must determine the functions of the governors, the principal, and the academic board in running the college. They must regulate the meetings of the governors and the academic board and their committees. They have to cover arrangements for appointing and dismissing staff, for student discipline, and for the appointment of a clerk to the governors.

Other sections deal in greater detail with the transfer of property (126) and staff (127) from the local authority to the new corporation, and for the dissolution of an HE corporation in the event of disaster or decline (128).

Funding councils

Designation of colleges within the PCFC sector is covered by Section 129.

New arrangements for funding higher education

131.—(1) There shall be established a body corporate to be known as the Universities Funding Council.

(2) The Council shall consist of fifteen members appointed by the Secretary of State, of whom one shall be so appointed as chairman.

(3) Not less than six and not more than nine of the members shall be persons appearing to the Secretary of State—

   (a) to have experience of, and to have shown capacity in, the provision of higher education; and

   (b) to be currently engaged in the provision of higher education:

and in appointing the remaining members the Secretary of State shall have regard to the desirability of including persons who appear to him to have experience of, and to have shown capacity in, industrial, commercial or financial matters or the practice of any profession ...

Sections 131 and 132 set up two bodies to distribute funds to higher education institutions: the Universities Funding Council (UFC) and the PCFC. The UFC has fifteen members including the chairman, appointed by the Secretary of State, 'not less than six and not more than nine' must be persons who have 'shown capacity in the provision of higher education' and who are 'currently engaged in the provision of higher education'. In appointing the remainder, the Secretary of State has to 'have regard to' the desirability of getting people with skill and experience in industry, commerce and finance.

132.—(1) There shall be established a body corporate to be known as the Polytechnics and Colleges Funding Council.

(2) The Council shall consist of fifteen members appointed by the Secretary of State, of whom one shall be so appointed as chairman.

(3) Not less than six and not more than nine of the members shall be persons appearing to the Secretary of State—

    (a) to have experience of, and to have shown capacity in, the provision of higher education; and

    (b) to be currently engaged in the provision of higher education;

and in appointing the remaining members the Secretary of State shall have regard to the desirability of including persons who appear to him to have experience of, and to have shown capacity in, industrial, commercial or financial matters or the practice of any profession ...

Activities of the UFC include advising the Secretary of State and distributing money to the universities for the purpose of education and research, and providing facilities for these activities. The council can make grants 'subject to such terms and conditions as they think fit'. Schedule 8 of the Act requires the UFC to have separate Committees for Wales and Scotland.

The PCFC has a similar composition: fifteen members, including the chairman, with a similar mix of academic and business experience. As well as having to provide for education and research in PCFC institutions, the Council has the power to provide for some higher education courses in local authority colleges of further education.

In making grants to institutions in support of the activities which come within its responsibilities, the PCFC can (like the UFC) attach certain conditions to the grant of funds. In keeping 'activities' under review, they can collect such information as they require, from local authorities and governors.

In Section 134, the Act confers on the Secretary of State the power to impose further duties on the Councils by Order. If a university or college fails to comply with the conditions which a Council attaches to any payment, all or some of the money can be reclaimed with interest.

134.—(3) The terms and conditions on which either of the Funding Councils make any grants or other payments may include in particular conditions—

    (a) enabling the Council to require the repayment, in whole or in part, of sums paid by the Council if any other condition subject to which the sums were paid is not complied with; and

    (b) requiring the payment of interest in respect of any period during which a sum due to the Council in accordance with any other condition remains unpaid:

but shall not relate to the application by the body to whom the grants or other payments are made of any sums derived otherwise than from the Council. . . .

(6) Subject to subsection (7) below, the Secretary of State may make grants to each of the Funding Councils of such amounts and subject to such conditions as he may determine.

(7) The conditions subject to which grants are made by the Secretary of State to either of the Funding Councils shall not relate to the making of grants or other payments by the Council to any specified institution.

(8) In exercising their functions under this Part of this Act each of the Funding Councils shall comply with any directions given to them by the Secretary of State.

Subsection (6) empowers the Secretary of State to attach conditions to the money he makes available to the Funding Councils, but subsection (7) prohibits him from making these conditions so explicit as to relate to the payment of a grant to any specified institution. Funding councils are obliged to comply with any directions which the Secretary of State may give them, but, to be valid, such directions must be made in the form of an Order laid before Parliament. The Councils are not permitted to attach conditions to the use of funds universities and colleges may raise from other sources.

The National Advisory Body for Public Sector Higher Education (NAB) is replaced by the Polytechnics and Colleges Funding Council. Section 136 transfers the residual assets from NAB to the PCFC, and enables the Secretary of State to designate employees of NAB for transfer to the staff of the PCFC.

Academic tenure and academic freedom

It is convenient to insert here a reference to the provisions in the Act on Academic Tenure which appear at Sections 202 to 208 under a 'Miscellaneous and General' heading.

One of the aims of the promoters of the Education Reform Act was to end academic tenure for new academic appointments. It was decided, therefore, to appoint five University Commissioners whose task it would be to revise the statutes of each university with this end in view.

Section 202 sets up the University Commissioners. Sections 203 to 205 and Schedule 11 lay down their functions and procedures. As drafted, the Bill imposed on the Commissioners a duty to 'have regard to the need:

(a) to enable qualifying institutions (that is, the universities and colleges coming under their review) to provide education, promote learning and engage in research efficiently and economically; and
(b) to apply the principles of justice and fairness.'

These now appear in the Act as Section 202(2)(b) and (c). In front of them is a new (2)(a) inserted by an amendment carried in the House of Lords, proposed by Lord Jenkins of Hillhead, Chancellor of the University of Oxford. It reads as follows:

(a) to ensure that academic staff have freedom within the law to question and test received wisdom, and put forward new ideas and controversial or unpopular opinions, without placing themselves in jeopardy of losing their jobs or privileges they may have . . .'

Section 203 defines the Commissioners' job. It is to amend the statutes so as to enable universities and colleges 'to dismiss any member of the academic staff by reason of redundancy' or 'for good cause', and to establish appeals procedures to deal with such cases.

Redundancy occurs when 'the institution has ceased or intends to cease' to carry on the activity for which a member of staff was appointed, or when the need to employ staff to do 'work of a particular kind' ceases or is expected to cease or diminish.

'Good cause' includes reasons related to a member of staff's capability or qualifications – i.e. if a member of staff is deemed to be inadequately competent or not qualified to do what is needed.

Section 204 empowers the Commissioners to modify the statutes of qualifying institutions 'as they consider necessary', in respect of all new appointments and promotions made 'on or after 20th November, 1987'.

The new appeals procedures would remove the need for a university or college Visitor to hear appeals. Section 206 therefore excludes the Visitor from intervening unless a specific function for him or her has been included in the revised appeals procedures.

All changes initiated by the Commissioners have to be approved by the Privy Council before coming into effect (Section 207).

Background

The Government's aims in bringing forward this part of the Act were set out some months before the Bill was published in a White Paper *Higher Education: Meeting the Challenge* (1987). The opening words of the foreword signed by Mr Kenneth Baker and his Cabinet colleagues for Scotland, Wales and Northern Ireland spelled the message out clearly:

> 'Higher education has a crucial role in helping the nation to meet the economic and social challenges of the final decade of this century and beyond . . . Higher education should:
> - serve the country more effectively
> - pursue basic scientific research and scholarship in the arts and humanities
> - have closer links with industry and commerce and promote enterprise.'

Chapter One of the White Paper went on to elaborate these headlines:

> 'The Government takes a wide view of the aims and purposes of higher education. It adheres to the Robbins Committee's definition: instruction in skills, the promotion of the general powers of the mind, the advancement of learning, and the transmission of a common culture and commons standards of citizenship. It fully recognises the value of research, and especially basic research, together with those areas of learning and scholarship which have at most an indirect relationship to the world of work . . .
>
> 'The Government believes that the British system of higher education is among the best in the world, both in the

quality of its research and of its graduates. But no area of our national life can afford to rest on past achievement . . . In higher education . . . there is a need to pursue reforms, both in the management and funding of the system and in the monitoring of the quality of its work, so that we can build on areas of excellence in the arts and sciences and social sciences. But above all there is an urgent need, in the interests of the nation as a whole, and therefore of universities, polytechnics and colleges themselves, for higher education to take increasing account of the economic requirements of the country.

'Meeting the needs of the economy is not the sole purpose of higher education nor can higher education alone achieve what is needed. But this aim, with its implications for the scale and quality of higher education, must be vigorously pursued . . .

'The Government and its central funding agencies will do all they can to encourage and reward approaches by higher education institutions which bring them close to the world of business. . . . '

Other paragraphs applied the same principles to research, promising that the research councils would protect basic research, but give greater priority to 'better targeted effort' yielding better value for money in terms of commercial exploitation.

The more the White Paper stressed the traditional academic and professional functions of higher education, the clearer became the overriding priority: universities and colleges had to be made to serve the Government's dominant aims for the success of British industry and commerce and the creation of an enterprise society.

The priority was unambiguous: 'above all' was the commitment to the economy, and there was, in the last sentence of the quoted passage, the clear intention to allocate resources in such a way as to reward those who cooperated, and penalise those who refused to do so.

The legislative changes, then, have to be seen in the light of this statement of intent. They are designed to provide the government of the day with the power to mobilise the resources of higher education in ways that they believe (or hope) will increase national wealth.

The reason why proposals in the Education Reform Bill were so highly controversial, and so deeply offensive to the university community at all levels, is to be found in the way relations between these institutions and the State had been conducted over the previous century. The British tradition had stressed the autonomy of the universities and their freedom from State direction. Continental universities and state universities in the United States might, in varying degree, be dependent on the political will of ministers and governments. In Britain the prestige of the universities was bound up in their autonomy, hedged around by Royal charters and the right to confer their own degrees.

The British universities had managed to retain a great deal of this autonomy in spite of becoming increasingly dependent on the State for the funding of both teaching and research. There had been a kind of benign conspiracy to preserve their respectable irresponsibility. Governments had connived in it by giving their benediction to an intermediate institution, the University Grants Committee, which allowed the universities to retain an arms-length relationship with the Treasury (and later, the Department of Education and Science). When the first grants from public funds were paid to university colleges in 1889 'a small committee of men well-versed in academic questions' was set up to distribute the money. Thirty years later, the University Grants Committee came into being with an extended role and larger funds, and in 1946 the arrangements were again reviewed, overhauled and confirmed.

While the sums of money and the student numbers were small, there was little need to think deeply about how universities fitted into the range of national priorities. Universities were taken for granted as institutions which did not need to be justified in principle. Academic freedom thrived on the universities' loose links with the State. Even so, in the aftermath of the Second World War decisions had to be taken about the expansion of the universities which brought them closer to the centre of public policy. The issue then, as now, was scientific manpower. What needed to be done to ensure a sufficient supply of qualified manpower in science and science-related professions? The matter was considered by the Barlow Committee which in 1946 recommended a doubling of the output of university science departments, and (almost as an afterthought) went outside its terms of reference to advocate a doubling of other university faculties as well. The form of words used in the report is revealing:

> 'We would deprecate any attempt to meet the increased demand for scientists and technologists at the expense of students of other subjects (even if, as is unlikely, the universities could be persuaded to make such an attempt) . . .'.

The implication was that the universities could only be 'persuaded', and Sir Alan Barlow, a senior Treasury mandarin, went along with this hypothesis even though the power of the purse was there to change it.

But as the magnitude of the universities' public subsidy increased, it was only a matter of time before these policy questions would become more pressing and contentious. Scientific and technological manpower remained a matter of public concern. Between 1954 and 1962, the Committee on Scientific Manpower chaired by Lord (then Sir Solly) Zuckerman strove to find the key to manpower planning in a series of inconclusive reports, before coming down firmly on the side of scepticism – a scepticism which the Robbins Committee echoed in 1963. Lord Crowther-Hunt, a Labour junior minister in the DES, tried again in the mid-1970s and had no more success.

But behind the fascination with manpower planning were questions which have now become very familiar: how can the universities be made to be useful to the nation? How can the concentration of talent in the universities be focused on ending the long-term decline in the British economy? And along with these questions went others which also demanded an answer: if this focus were to be sharpened, how could the other traditional functions of universities be guaranteed? How could they continue to be places of independent scholarship and criticism? How much independence of thought and freedom of scholarship is tolerable to a government in a hurry, beset by short-term economic pressures?

So long as the conventional wisdom which emphasised the universities' autonomy ruled out direct government intervention, governments could only rely on exhortation and the power of argument. And if truth were told, the argument for intervention was always blunted by the suspicion that ministers and civil servants had no better idea of what universities should be doing than had university teachers and vice-chancellors.

The crisis which precipitated a change came in 1981, when harsh cuts in public expenditure impinged with particular severity on the universities because of their direct dependence on cash-limited Treasury grants.

The 1981 squeeze tested to destruction the principle of arms-length funding. The University Grants Committee, a body which university professors dominated, distributed the cuts according to their own assessments of merit. Those universities which were hardest hit included places like Aston and Salford which had made the greatest efforts to establish links with industry and to tailor courses to the demands of industrialists and businessmen. The cuts were not so distributed out of perversity, but because the UGC applied the values of the international academic community rather than those of the Department of Trade and Industry.

A new planning and funding system

What emerged from the 1981 crisis was a stronger role for the DES, and clearer, published guidelines for the UGC. There was also a recognition that if the Government wanted to impose a different set of priorities on the universities, it would have to look at the mechanism for the distribution of funds and try to create one which would be relied upon to work with the grain of Government policy, not against it.

The result was the decision to scrap the UGC and replace it with the Universities Funding Council, on which representatives of industry, commerce and the professions would play a larger part with the academics losing their built-in majority.

The Act made it clear that this body would receive clear instructions from the Secretary of State, to whom it would be responsible, and that it, in its turn, would make payments to universities on terms and conditions which would have to be complied with. The formula is that of a customer who contracts with a supplier for the provision of services. Universities are to be paid for services rendered. If the services are not rendered in accordance with the contract, they are not entitled to be paid and must refund any cash which has been received in advance.

The sections (131–134) which spell out the powers of the funding councils have to be read in parallel with the White Paper and the DES memoranda, to understand the full measure of the change and the full extent of the powers which the central Government has taken to control higher education.

The role of the civil servants in the DES is much enhanced, as is that of the officials of the funding councils. Policies will have to be developed at the national level on a range of matters hitherto left to the universities to decide for themselves. Accountability will demand more and more attention to prescribed performance indicators and the monitoring of output information. It now becomes the task of the DES, along with (and probably led by) the Department of Trade and Industry, the Department of Employment and the Treasury, to shape policy for higher education to meet the Government's main economic and social objectives, and to create the bureaucracy needed to ensure that this is carried through.

It is difficult to exaggerate the magnitude of the change in the management of British higher education implicit in these sections of the Act. One set of long-standing conventions has been swept away. The foundations have shifted. The idea of universities as independent centres of learning and research, capable of standing out against government and society, and offering critical judgements of varying objectivity, informed by learning and protected by the autonomy of historic institutions, is discarded. Instead universities are made the servants of the State and its priorities. In the context of the late twentieth century they, like the rest of the education system, are to be used in the attempt to create a nation of enterprise and to discredit the 'dependency culture' associated with the forty years after World War Two.

Academic freedom is still an ideal to honour and scholarship remains one, but only one, of the objects of higher education. By changing the method of funding, the Act goes to the heart of the power relationship between higher education and the government. For nearly a century governments have struggled to insulate universities from political pressure. Now policy has been stood on its head. Universities are to be paid for doing what the Government tells them to do, or not paid at all.

These questions took up a lot of time and energy when the Bill was debated in Parliament, and particularly in the House of Lords, where the universities were well represented by present and former university dons, and by noble university chancellors.

Late in the House of Lords Committee stage, the protagonists of the universities succeeded in carrying an amendment aimed at limiting the power of the UFC to put conditions on the payments it makes to institutions. The aim was to attack the principle of funding by 'contract'. The Bill itself was silent on the matter of contracts, but by making Funding Councils dependent on the Secretary of State's instructions, and the universities dependent on the strings which the UFC attached to any money paid out, it laid the groundwork for the kind of contracting system outlined earlier in the White Paper.

The Government refused to accept the Lords amendment. When the Bill went back to the House of Commons, Mr Baker restored the essential powers which the amendment had aimed to undermine. There was some softening of the language – 'grants' instead of 'payments' – and it was agreed that the Secretary of State should not intervene to tell the UFC how to treat individual institutions.

The original draft of the Bill had restricted the activities of the Funding Councils to the distribution of funds in accordance with the Secretary of State's guidance. This was intended to make it clear that the new Universities Funding Council should not have the wider advisory role which had been assumed by the University Grants Committee. An amendment in the House of Lords challenged this and succeeded in writing back into the Act provision for the UFC to 'provide the Secretary of State, in such manner as he may from time to time determine, with such information and advice relating to activities eligible for funding . . . as they think fit'. This still leaves the Secretary of State in a strong position to control the UFC agenda. But the Lords' amendment (Section 134(8)) ensured that any directions issued by the Secretary of State to the Funding Councils must be made in the form of an Order laid before Parliament.

There are many reasons for believing that the Government itself is uncertain about how the contract system will work. But the firmness with which the universities' amendments were resisted made it clear that the Government was determined to change the ground rules and bring about a radical shift in the balance of power in higher education. An increase in uncertainty was one element in the process of achieving this.

As soon as the Act became law Ministers began to recognise the irony of an Administration which favoured market-based decision-making, adopting a *dirigiste* attitude towards higher education. From the autumn of 1988, the emphasis changed and the funding councils were encouraged to look for ways of distributing money which would reward institutional entrepreneurship, and decentralised decisions.

Changes in the basis of the recurrent grant – increasing the fee element – were intended to give universities and colleges more opportunity to capitalise on their own success. Higher education vouchers again surfaced as a possible way of distributing money to institutions via their clients rather than in the form of State subventions. The *dirigiste* powers remained on the Statute Book while the higher education community learned to live with the new regime.

The immediate effect was to increase the incentives for universities and colleges to admit additional students. Unit costs came down (in real terms) while numbers went up and the proportion of the age group entering higher education rose by more than a third to approach 25 per cent. It showed that the hitherto suppressed demand was sufficient to maintain an expansion of numbers even though the demographic trend was downwards.

Polytechnics and colleges

The Act set up two funding councils with similar composition, one for the universities, one for the polytechnics and colleges. The Universities Funding Council attracted most of the comment when the Bill was passing through Parliament, but the provisions for what used to be known as the 'public sector' of higher education also marked a clear departure from past practice, and a tightening of the Government's grip.

The Education Reform Act provided the opportunity radically to reduce the participation of the local authorities in higher education. The Polytechnics and Colleges Funding Council took over responsibility for the planning and financing of higher education in the public sector colleges, and under its aegis the colleges themselves were required to become independent, self-governing, higher education corporations.

These changes were in line with other parts of the Act, designed to reduce the local authority influence. The Government believed that if strategic decisions about the planning of courses and the allocation of resources were taken nationally, each college could then be allowed to stand on its own feet with its own autonomous board of governors. The governors and the senior academic staff, would then be encouraged to act like entrepreneurs, managing their college in response to the policy signals and cash incentives emanating from the funding council and from local industry. There would be no role in this for the local authorities.

The local authorities campaigned against the change, but without much heart. A few years before (1982) they had successfully ridden out an attempt to make similar changes. The outcome on that occasion had been the setting up of the National Advisory Body for Public Sector Higher Education, which represented a working compromise between central and local government. With a strong professional secretariat, NAB gave the local authorities a major role in the planning process, while reserving the final decisions to the Secretary of State. This seemed to work pretty well, so long as the Secretary of State and his representative, the junior minister with responsibility for higher education, were prepared to enter into the spirit of the enterprise and take the local education authorities seriously – even if this meant, on occasion exercising normal political arts of persuasion and cajolery. By the time the White Paper on higher education was in preparation, the writing was on the wall for local government. Ministers had ceased to conceal their impatience with NAB and their contempt for the local authorities' advice on higher education policy.

The colleges of higher education run by voluntary bodies, including the Church colleges, are also brought under the aegis of the PCFC. They welcomed this, but were at the same time somewhat apprehensive that they might lose the inside track to the DES which they had enjoyed when they constituted a block of direct grant institutions in a world of local authority colleges.

An amendment to the first draft of the Bill was intended to allay fears that they might lose ground when brought under the PCFC umbrella.

It occurs at Section 132(9), which requires the PCFC to:

> 'have regard (so far as they think it appropriate to do so, in the light of any other relevant considerations) to the desirability of maintaining what appears to them to be for the time being an appropriate balance in their support of . . . activities as between institutions . . . which are of a denominational character and other institutions so concerned.'

The paragraph managed to combine every weasel phrase: 'have regard to . . . as they think it appropriate . . . in the light of other relevant considerations . . . for the time being . . . an appropriate balance . . .'. It stands out as a classic example of cautious and almost meaningless wording inserted in an Act in a not very determined effort to placate a not very powerful pressure group.

Division of responsibility

[Note: The paragraphs which follow refer to Sections of the Act which proved to be short-lived. In the spring of 1991, the Government published a White Paper which led to the 1992 Higher and Further Education Act which removed further education from the sphere of the local authorities and financed it through funding councils, similar to those which provide funds for the universities, polytechnics and other colleges of higher education. See note on page 104.]

The local authority responsibility for further education was now defined as a statutory duty (Section 120). The relevant sections of the 1944 Education Act were obsolete. These prescribed certain procedures local authorities had to follow: for example, they had to prepare and keep up to date further education schemes, approved by the central government. All or most of the authorities produced such plans in the late 1940s and early 1950s, but the plans had not been kept up to date. To have done so would have been costly in time and effort, both at the local and the national level, and there was a silent acceptance that these bureaucratic hurdles could be dispensed with. Had any officious guardians of legal niceties chosen to test matters in the Courts it might have been necessary to introduce an Indemnity Bill, but this did not happen.

The local authorities retained the power to provide higher education in certain circumstances to meet the needs of their areas. It was clearly intended that most courses of higher education would be provided in colleges funded by the Polytechnics and Colleges Funding Council, and the PCFC was also expected to 'contract' with local authorities to continue certain higher education courses in colleges maintained by local authorities. That would occur in colleges which straddled the two systems – those which do not do enough higher education work to be brought into the PCFC sector, but which still continue to provide some advanced courses alongside the bulk of their further education work.

Local authorities also had the power to finance some higher education courses of their own. This was intended to cover mainly part-time, non-degree courses, designed to meet local, rather than national, needs.

Definition of further education
Further education is now more clearly defined as 'full-time and part-time education and training for persons over compulsory school age, other than higher education, and any related organised leisure-time occupation'. The definition breaks new ground in insisting that to qualify as further education within the meaning of the Act, an 'organised leisure-time occupation' must be one which is provided 'in connection with' further education and training. This restricts the range of permissible provisions in ways which have yet to be tested. The technical reason why this provision was thought to be necessary was that some limitation had to replace the controls which had theoretically been avail-

able under the obsolete 1944 Act schemes of further education. It is probably intended to be no more than a safeguard against 'under-water basket weaving' or whatever is shorthand for the ultimate absurdity.

College management

The sections which deal with arrangements for PCFC colleges to become higher education corporations reflect the other side of the coin labelled 'centralisation'. Having set up a national system of controlling spending and allocating resources, the Act then sets out to decentralise control to the institutions and increase the colleges' capacity to bring forward their own local initiatives. These depend heavily on strong governing bodies and presuppose energetic and time-consuming participation by local businessmen. There may well have been an overestimation of the readiness and ability of lay men and women to engage fruitfully in this work. The provisions of self-government were a logical development of the arrangements already in place. The difference is that the colleges themselves will gain control over the budgets remitted to them (or contracted by them) via PCFC, instead of being told by the local authority how much they can spend.

Academic tenure and academic freedom

The decision to end academic tenure, where this was provided by university statutes, had been signalled during Sir Keith Joseph's period of office as Secretary of State for Education and Science. It was felt that the requirements of good management made it necessary for university authorities to be able to review their staffing arrangements and match them to immediate objectives and obligations. This meant being able to decide that particular departments or sub-departments were no longer needed, or could only be sustained on a smaller scale. In managerial terms, 'tenure' – a career-long freehold in an office – made it difficult to bring about rapid changes of direction or reductions in expenditure.

The crisis of 1981 and subsequent provisions for early retirement and restructuring had drawn attention to the wide variety of tenure provisions in the charters and statutes of the institutions of higher education. Some universities like Oxford and Cambridge had very strong guarantees of tenure till retiring age. Others – including some distinguished universities like Bristol – had statutes which made it quite possible, legally, to dismiss redundant staff.

What this pointed to was that academic tenure was even more important as an unchallenged idea than as a legal entitlement. Universities, and colleges in the public sector, acted as if tenure were a reality even when it was not.

The method of proceeding – the setting up of a University Commission charged with the review of each individual university's Charter – followed established precedent. It was argued that the antiquity of some university studies, and the need to take adequate account of the particular circumstances of varied institutions, made this the only satisfactory way to tackle the questions of academic tenure.

Tenure as a concept was closely linked to academic freedom. The university don's freehold, like the parson's, was regarded as protection against gagging or victimisation for advancing unpopular beliefs, thinking dangerous thoughts, or pursuing unwelcome research into sensitive matters. The dispute which arose when the Bill came to Parliament concerned the search for a form of words which, in ending tenure, would nevertheless restate and defend the principle of academic freedom.

This was the object of the Jenkins amendment, which wrote into the instructions to the Commissioners the specific requirement to 'have regard to the need' to defend academic freedom.

The Lord Chancellor, who spoke on this for the Government, opposed the amendment because of its imprecision and doubtful value, except as a declaration of goodwill. But it was carried against his advice because peers recognised the importance of the issue and wanted to do something, even if they could do little more than make a gesture in the direction of academic freedom.

6

Finance and Government of Locally Funded Further and Higher Education

Sections 139 to 155

The aim of these sections was to apply to local authority further education colleges similar principles of financial delegation and self-government which were elsewhere applied to schools.

This legislation was replaced by the relevant sections of the Higher and Further Education Act, 1992 to which reference has already been made. The Act removed the colleges of further education and sixth form colleges from the local authority sector, turned them into charitable corporations run by their own boards of governors, and financed them through a Further Education Funding Council on the lines already established for higher education. The Act reached the Statute Book shortly before Parliament was dissolved for the 1992 general election. It had been fiercely contested and it was recognized that these clauses would depend for their implementation on the outcome of the election.

What follows in the rest of this chapter is a summary of the short-lived provisions of the Education Reform Act on the finance and governance of further education, with a discussion of the background.

Schemes of delegation

Every local authority must prepare a scheme for the Secretary of State's approval (Section 139) showing how the authority's further education is to be divided up between its colleges. Such a scheme must cover an authority's maintained colleges and the handful of 'assisted' colleges of further and higher education. In respect of all colleges with 200 or more full-time students, control over the 'budget share' must be delegated to college governors (Section 142). Authorities may, if they think fit and/or the Secretary of State determines, extend delegation to colleges with fewer than 200 full-time students (Section 144) and to adult education centres (Section 146).

Further and higher education funding schemes

139.—(1) It shall be the duty of every local education authority to prepare a scheme in accordance with this Chapter and submit it for the approval of the Secretary of ·State in accordance with section 140 of this Act.

(2) The scheme shall provide for—

(a) the determination in respect of each financial year of the authority, for each institution required to be covered by the scheme in that year, of the share to be appropriated for that institution in that year of the further and higher education budget of the authority for that year (referred to below in this Chapter, in relation to such an institution, as the institution's budget share); and

(b) the delegation by the authority of the management of an institution's budget share for any year to the governing body of the institution where such delegation is required or permitted by or under the scheme.

In drawing up schemes, local authorities must set out the 'principles and procedures' to be applied by the authority in planning the provision which the colleges are to be expected to make.

Section 140 gives the Secretary of State power to lay down the procedures for the preparation and submission of schemes and issue guidance which local authorities must take into account. Section 140(4) obliges authorities to consult college governors when they prepare their schemes, which come into effect, when approved, from a date determined by the Secretary of State. Section 140(6) and (7) give him the power to impose his own scheme if the authority fails to act.

Provision is made for revising such schemes (Section 141), but allows that 'minor variations' can be made without formal submission. Major variations require an Order from the Secretary of State.

As with financial delegation to schools, local authorities are obliged to devise a 'formula' (Section 143) to govern the allocation to colleges, based on a weighted per capita share as set out in subsections (3) to (5). If the number of full-time equivalent students falls below 200, delegation is withdrawn. This figure can be lowered by regulation if the Secretary of State thinks this expedient.

A paragraph at the end of Section 144 – subsection (12) – enjoins the colleges to supply the local authority with such information as it requires for it to exercise its monitoring functions. The Act provides (Sections 145 and 146) for delegation to be phased in over several years.

The process of financial delegation is to be as open as it can be made.

Each local authority is required to publish its scheme in accordance with regulations (Section 147) as, and as often as, the Secretary of State lays down. There is a further requirement on local authorities to publish information about the operation of the scheme, in a form which the Secretary of State may prescribe.

Staffing
Delegation carries with it power for the governors over the appointment

---

152.—(1) The instrument of government of any institution to which section 151 of this Act applies shall provide for the governing body to consist of not more than twenty-five members selected and appointed or (as the case may be) co-opted in accordance with the instrument of government, of whom—

    (a) not less than fifty per cent. shall be members of one or other of the categories mentioned in subsection (2) below; and

    (b) not more than twenty per cent. shall be persons selected and appointed by the local education authority.

(2) The categories of members referred to in subsection (1)(a) above are—

    (a) members selected from among persons appearing to the person or persons selecting them—

        (i) to be, or to have been, engaged or employed in business industry or any profession or in any other field of employment relevant to the activities of the institution; or

        (ii) to represent persons so engaged or employed; and

    (b) members co-opted by the governing body.

(3) The instrument of government shall provide that persons who are—

    (a) members of, or of any committee or sub-committee of, any local authority or local education authority; or

    (b) employed by any local authority or local education authority; are disqualified for being members of the governing body of either category mentioned in subsection (2) above.

and dismissal of staff. The exercise of this power is subject to the Articles of Government of each college (which have to be approved by the Secretary of State) and is not regulated in detail by the terms of the Act. Section 148, however, covers staffing in general terms. It is for the governors to determine the complement of teaching and non-teaching staff, and to make all such appointments (Section 148(3)). The local authority continues to be the employer of the teachers, but 'it shall be the duty of the authority to appoint staff selected by the governing body', subject to basic eligibility on grounds of qualification. The chief education officer of the local authority is entitled to be consulted before any decision to hire or fire a senior member of staff (as defined in the college's Articles of Government) and, if invited, the CEO must advise on other appointments or staffing matters.

As in the case of schools, Section 148 provides for the cost of dismissals and premature retirements to be borne by the local authority, unless there is 'good reason' for the authority to charge the college. A 'no redundancy policy' is expressly ruled out (subsection 9) as a possible 'good reason'.

Withdrawal of powers
If the governors fail to do their job effectively, in the opinion of the local authority, or if the governors mismanage their budget, Section 150 lays down how the local authority can withdraw all or some of the delegated powers.

Articles of Government
The constitution for each governing body is provided by Instruments of Government made by the local authority, with the approval of the Secretary of State and subject to such conditions as he lays down (Sections 151 and 152). A governing body is to have not more than 25 members, of whom not more than 20 per cent are to be nominated by the local authority. Not less than half the governors are to be drawn from people who are, or have been, in business, industry, a profession, or some other relevant employment, or who represent such industrial or professional people; or co-opted members. Employees or members of local authorities or any of their committees cannot qualify as representatives of industry or commerce, or be co-opted members.

The Articles of Government must provide an outline of the governing body's committee structure and the college's academic board. It is for the local authority to make all the first appointments in governing bodies when they are reorganised along the lines laid down by the new Instruments and Articles of Government. In making these appointments, however, the local authority has complete power of selection only over the 20 per cent of members who are local authority representatives. The employer appointments are drawn from bodies representing business interests, professions, and trade unions, using lists of organisations drawn up locally and approved by the Secretary of State.

Separate sections (153 and 154) authorise the Secretary of State to make regulations about the government of the small number of local authority colleges of 'further and higher' education, which, if they acquire corporate status (see Chapter 5), become known not as 'maintained' but 'assisted'. The achievement of corporate status involves becoming a company limited by guarantee under the Companies Act, with a memorandum and articles of association which have to be consistent with the principles which apply either to the Polytechnics and Colleges Funding Council sector or to the local authority sector. Section 157 empowers the Secretary of State to modify Trust Deeds where this is necessary as a result of incorporation or otherwise and lays down procedures he must follow.

Section 158 gives the Secretary of State the power to call for returns of information from the governors of colleges in the PCFC and local authority sectors and from 'designated assisted' institutions providing full-time education.

Background

The decision to take the polytechnics and other colleges of advanced further and higher education away from the local authorities and hand them over to the Polytechnics and Colleges Funding Council, left the local authorities in England and Wales with some 400 further education colleges, attended by 1.8 million students, 93 per cent of them coming within the categories of non-advanced further education. Another 1.8 million students of all kinds were enrolled in adult education courses. All in all, the whole enterprise cost more than £1 billion a year (1987).

In the early 1990s, the colleges face the same demographic challenge which the primary and secondary schools have experienced in the 1980s. In 1994 there will be one-third fewer young people in the 16–19 age group than there were in 1983. Other changes which have overtaken the further education system include the increased part in planning and financing played by the then Manpower Services Commission and its institutional successors. By taking over responsibility for funding 25 per cent of work-related non-advanced further education, the Commission gained a powerful influence over the other 75 per cent. But as most of the intelligence about local needs on which decisions are made comes up through the colleges, the scope for initiative on the part of the further education institutions remains considerable. It is this initiative which, theoretically, financial delegation should foster.

Financial delegation

The sections of the Act dealing with delegated management to colleges are broadly in line with those for schools. The situation before 1988 was that the degree of delegation to colleges varied widely from place to place and college to college. What is now enacted is a more uniform and systematic regime.

The Act requires local authorities to prepare new schemes for further and higher education. By the time the Bill received the Royal Assent, the DES had issued a draft Circular detailing 47 items which authorities must cover in drawing up a scheme. Each authority must begin by showing how it intends, each year, to make a comprehensive plan for its provision for further and higher education. It has to take account of what is being provided by others – PCFC colleges, schools, private training institutions, other local authorities – and having done so, make its own priority plans. Then the authority has to translate these plans into allocations of funds for its colleges.

Local authorities must resist the temptation to concentrate all their resources on their own further education colleges, because they are also required to bear in mind the possible need to contract for some courses to be laid on in colleges in the PCFC sector. They must also have regard to provision in industry and in private institutions.

During the passage of the Bill there were serious doubts about the fate of the small number of surviving higher education courses in local authority colleges and the courses at sub-degree level in PCFC colleges. The intention was clear that there should continue to be traffic both ways across this new funding frontier. The extent to which this happens depends on how far the Act is successful in making local authorities, stripped of their day-to-day responsibilities for college management, concentrate on their strategic role.

Schemes prepared by authorities have to show how this planning function is to be carried out, in consultation with a wide variety of institutions and interests, including (prominently) the Training Commission, local industry and the colleges. Authorities have then to go on to explain a method by which the strategic plan can be translated into college budgets.

The Circular discussed at length the questions which arise in allocating weighted values to courses of different kinds in different colleges, at different levels and with different priorities. (Schedule 7 of the Act provides guidance on the calculation of full-time equivalent numbers on different modes of attendance.)

There is a clear difference between the approach to financial delegation at the school level and that in further education. Control over their budgets, for schools, is a means of increasing competition between institutions. Overlap and duplication is of the essence, with the weakest going to the wall and the strongest receiving additional resources. Planning by the local authority or the diocesan authorities is at a discount: it is for the market to decide where expansion takes place and which institutions fail. In further education, on the other hand, authority-wide planning by an efficient bureaucracy is the order of the day. The planners must consult and be responsive to demand, but when they have heard all the arguments they must make their decisions – give colleges their 'planned student numbers', courses by course, and a budget based on their weighted value. A college which successfully attracted more students than the budget allowed for would be assumed to have done so (according to the draft Circular) because it chose to do so, 'because it considers that they can be accommodated at zero or marginal cost within the budget'. It will not automatically receive extra contingency funds, though it may be well placed in the scramble for funds the following year. By the same token a college which fails to fill its places stands to lose money next time round. The Circular recognises that arrangements may have to be different for tertiary colleges where, presumably, a greater degree of competition is accepted.

As with the schools, the authorities have to incorporate the various weighted cost elements into a common formula so that their FE budgets can be distributed among the colleges on an open and rational basis. This also means deciding how much to hold back for 'excepted items' – capital spending, administrative and advisory services – and a diverse range of other costs which may include premature retirements, dismissals and other staff costs, an LEA development fund (for curriculum development, marketing, outreach and the like), an LEA contingency fund, DES specific grants, and any specific items an authority might seek the Secretary of State's agreement to exclude. There also has to be provision for transitional arrangements, to ensure that going over to a new formula does not have excessively severe consequences for some colleges at the point of change.

The Circular's treatment of the 'administrative and advisory services' item is indicative of future intentions. Various options are considered. All envisage the earmarking of funds, but with varying degrees of discretion for the college on how to use the money. Option E (which may be read as an ultimately preferred option) suggests that 'the LEA might include funds for a service within delegated budgets so that colleges had full discretion on how much to spend on it and when to obtain it'.

Governing bodies
The Act reduces the chances of local authority domination by limiting the representation by members or employees of local authorities. Such governors can only occupy up to 20 per cent of the 20–25 seats on the governing body. Originally it had been intended to insist that at least half the members should be representatives of industry and commerce. This was the proposal which appeared in the consultative document issued in August 1987. The response, however, convinced ministers that in colleges where a large proportion of the non-advanced further education consisted of work for GCSE and A level, it would be inappropriate for half the governors to represent employer interests.

The 50 per cent non-local authority membership required under Section 133, therefore, includes co-opted members drawn from 'constituencies' which are to be laid down in the individual Instrument of Government of each college.

The consultative document gave an illustration of how a 24-person governing body might be constituted:

12 representatives of industry, commerce, the
    professions, etc.
4 representatives from the local authority
2 representatives of parents
2 representatives of neighbouring local authorities
2 members of staff
1 student
1 principal

In the light of the final drafting of the Act, the twelve representatives of business might come down to eight or ten, with the
addition of some co-opted members with knowledge of secondary and higher education – but these could not be teachers in
maintained schools nor hold any other local authority appointment.

In the consultative document, the Government had proposed
that the chairman of the governing body of a college of further
education should always be drawn from the ranks of non-local
authority members:

> 'Given the importance of bolstering the position of govern-
> ing bodies as an independent force clearly distinct from both
> the local education authority and the college, it would not
> be appropriate for a local education authority nominee or a
> representative of the staff or the students to chair the
> governing body.'

But here again, second thoughts prevailed. This stipulation
did not appear in the Bill and, though the Government would
like to see many employer representatives presiding over
governing bodies, the Act is silent on the subject.

Powers

Governing bodies will have wide powers to manage their colleges within the budget allocation which they receive and in
accordance with the strategies laid down by the local authority
and the Department of Employment.

A major part of the responsibility of governing bodies will be
the approval and supervision of the college budget, within the
sum allocated by the local authority. The intention is to give

them full powers of virement – that is, switching funds from one heading to another in the course of the budget period – and to enable them (unusually) to carry funds saved in one year, over to the next. They are to have the right to stop using local authority services if they think they can get a better deal by contracting with another provider. The consultative document emphasised the need to allow colleges to hold or retain part, at least, of any earnings which accrued from services provided by the college for payment on a full-cost basis.

Staffing
Governors' powers extend to all matters of staffing, subject to consultation with the chief education officer or his nominees on senior appointments and on dismissals. Procedures laid down in the schemes prepared by local authorities and in the Articles of Government of individual colleges will have to be followed – as, for example, when vacancies occur in an area where there are teachers available for redeployment – and the local authority will have the right to put forward candidates for consideration before or at the same time as a post is advertised.

In practice, also, the governors' powers in personnel matters will be limited by what the consultative document called a 'framework agreed with the local education authority'; and 'financial delegation would not affect the basic framework and provisions of agreements, national and local, currently in force on pay and conditions for college staff'. Subject to this big proviso, governors will be able to fix their own staff complements and grading for teaching and non-teaching staff.

7

Education in Inner London

Sections 162 to 196

The aim of these sections was to abolish the Inner London Education Authority and to make the inner London boroughs the education authorities for the population within their boundaries. Many of the clauses were of a technical nature, relating to the transfer of property, staff and residual obligations.

The principles behind this part of the Act were clear. Education in London was to become the responsibility of the boroughs, as it is the responsibility of the counties, metropolitan districts and outer London boroughs, and the legislation was drafted to bring this about by 1 April 1990, the date written into Section 162 which abolished the Inner London Education Authority and the 'Inner London Education Area' over which its writ had formerly run. This is the area covered by twelve inner London boroughs and the City of London, which Section 163 elevated to the status of local education authorities.

Reorganisation of provision of education in inner London
162.—(1) On 1st April 1990 the following shall cease to exist—

  (a) the Inner London Education Authority (in this Part referred to as "ILEA") and any education committee established by that Authority; and

  (b) the Inner London Educational Area. . . .

163.—(1) On the abolition date each inner London council shall become the local education authority for its area. . . .

(2) In this Part, "inner London council" means the council of an inner London borough or (in their capacity as a local authority) the Common Council of the City of London.

The London Residuary Body (set up in connection with the abolition of the Greater London Council under the 1985 Local Government Act) received a new remit, extending its life and giving it responsibilities arising from the disposal of property and assets of the former ILEA. (Later Sections 176 to 187 dealt in detail with these powers and responsibilities, which include dealing with redundancy and compensation, pensions, property, the ILEA's final accounts and other financial transactions with the boroughs; and with the final winding up of the Residuary Body itself and the disposal of its contracts and liabilities.)

Other sections (188–191) prevent the ILEA from disposing of property or entering into contracts involving more than £15000 without the permission of the Secretary of State, or otherwise acting to frustrate the transfer of responsibilities and assets to the boroughs.

To enable the transfer of responsibility to the boroughs to take place in an orderly fashion, Section 165 required the inner London councils to prepare and publish development plans showing how they intended to carry out the functions of a local education authority. Section 165(2) specified some of the basic provisions which such plans had to incorporate – for example, all the ILEA properties which it was intended to take over, and any ILEA schools located elsewhere which it was planned to continue to maintain had to be listed. The Section put strong emphasis on consultation, on the need to pay attention to the Secretary of State's statutory guidance, and on the obligation to publish the details of the scheme widely to give all concerned the opportunity to express a view. It would then be for the Secretary of State to make an Order under Section 166 detailing exactly which schools the new education authority should take over – that is, which county and voluntary schools would be maintained by the new authorities, or which grant-maintained schools would also become eligible for certain general services provided by the boroughs. All ILEA school governors ceased to hold office at the abolition date (Section 167). Section 168 empowers the Secretary of State to transfer the 'property, rights and liabilities' which went with the take-over; in certain circumstances the transfer could be to local authorities outside inner London.

Staff

Following procedures adopted when the Greater London Council was abolished, the Act sets up a Staff Commission (Section 170) 'to advise the Secretary of State on the steps necessary to safeguard the interests of the staff employed by the relevant authorities in so far as they are affected by the abolition of the ILEA'. This means keeping under review recruitment by the new education authorities and the arrangements for the transfer of staff. The Commission has a duty to follow DES direction on procedure and in other matters. ILEA staff salaries are specifically covered by Section 171, which was aimed at stopping the dying ILEA from bumping up salaries in such a way as to create additional financial claims on the successor bodies or the London Residuary Body.

Under Section 169 the Secretary of State acquires certain powers over the management structure to be set up by each inner borough as far as education is concerned, during the first five years after the abolition of the ILEA. In particular, the boroughs must consult him on the appointment of a chief education officer and any other senior official he may designate. If he thinks the borough's nominee is not a 'fit person' he can forbid the appointment.

A large-scale transfer of staff from the ILEA to the boroughs is envisaged in Section 172, which gives the Secretary of State the power to transfer contracts of employment without termination, 'as if' the original contract had been between the staff member and the new employer (Section 172(2)). A staff member would still retain the right to terminate the contract of employment if 'a substantial change is made to his detriment in his working conditions'. For such staff the compensation payable is as laid down in regulations made under the Superannuation Act of 1972. (The intention is to apply the terms used at the time of the abolition of the GLC.)

The process of transferring the functions of the ILEA to the boroughs made it necessary to require the ILEA to provide a great deal of detailed information (Section 166) to the other councils and the London Residuary Body. Section 195 also aims to smooth the process of transition by reasserting the validity of actions taken by the ILEA before the abolition date, and by asserting that 'anything which at that date is in process of being done by . . . ILEA . . . which become functions of the inner London councils . . . or of the London Residuary Body may be continued by . . . the successor authority' (Section 195(2)).

Background

The organisation and structure of the education service in the inner London area has been a matter of debate ever since 1870.

The decision to abolish the Inner London Education Authority came about by a combination of circumstances which forced the Government's hand. The election manifesto presented by the Conservatives before the 1987 General Election proposed an opt-out scheme for the boroughs which fell short of outright abolition:

'In the area covered by the Inner London Education Authority where entire borough councils wish to become independent of the l.e.a. they will be able to submit proposals to the Secretary of State requesting permission to take over the provision of education within their boundaries.'

This commitment was seen as a way of letting Conservative-controlled boroughs, like Wandsworth, Westminster and Kensington and Chelsea, break away from the ILEA without confronting the political and intellectual difficulties implicit in full-blooded abolition and the transfer of responsibility to the inner boroughs.

What happened, however, did not follow the manifesto. Having won the election, the Conservative Government inserted its break-away clause in the draft Bill. It immediately became apparent that the prospect of certain boroughs opting out would destabilise the ILEA. A long drawn-out period of uncertainty and decline was all that the ILEA school system could look forward to. The eventual completion of the dismemberment was envisaged in the Bill, which laid down that as soon as eight boroughs had 'opted out', the Secretary of State would be empowered to deliver the *coup de grâce* and finish off the ILEA.

At the Committee stage in the House of Commons, two powerful ex-ministers, Mr Michael Heseltine and Mr Norman Tebbit, joined forces to move an amendment which replaced the opting-out clause with a simple proposal for immediate abolition and transfer. Faced with the prospect of defeat at the hands of their own back benchers, ministers bowed to the inevitable and submitted their own amendments along these lines.

In the House of Lords, a last-ditch attempt to get a more rational consideration of London's needs and how to meet them, was mounted by the Bishop of London, Lord Kilmarnock (SDP) and Lord Annan (Independent). It failed in the face of an exceptionally large turn-out of Government supporters.

The result of this sequence of events was to force through a 'solution' to London education which few people inside the Government or outside would have advocated at the time of the 1987 election.

The Inner London Education Authority stood accused by its critics of three principal failings:

- excessive size, remoteness and bureaucracy
- poor educational standards
- extravagance and inefficiency.

The first line of criticism – the size and unwieldy nature of the London education system – was implicit in the original 1870 decision to base the organisation of education in London on the 113 square miles which formed the territory of the old Metropolitan Board of Works. Even in 1870 this was a contentious issue. The original plan was to divide London up into smaller areas, using the workhouse school districts and vestry boundaries, but W. E. Forster, the architect of the 1870 Act, was overtaken by a Commons revolt which brought the large metropolitan authority into being.

The London School Board enjoyed high prestige, recruited many eminent members and became recognised early as a forward-looking and energetic body with the resources – financial, intellectual and administrative – to tackle the formidable social and educational challenge of the London slums. It expected to think in terms of a high-quality, large-scale enterprise, and within ten years, it had already established a pattern of expenditure which made the unit costs of London elementary schools half as high again as the national average. (Matthew Arnold, writing as an HMI in 1878, castigated London's extravagance in spending 53s 3d per pupil, compared with 35s 3d elsewhere.)

But political tensions were already apparent. The London School Board elections tended to be won by the Progressives; the Moderates spent many years in opposition. In 1902, when the School Boards were abolished and most of the responsibility for education passed to the counties and country boroughs, London was the subject of a separate Bill.

The mantle did not pass to the London County Council without lengthy debate and lively intrigue, and a strong Conservative attempt to break up the London education service on the grounds that it was too big and bureaucratic. A suggested alternative was for a two-tier arrangement in which power would be shared with the boroughs. In the end the London County Council (and Mr Sydney Webb) triumphed, and took over where the London School Board and the Technical Education Board had left off.

The LCC's sixty-year rule saw the creation of the modern London education system – the rise, first, of the grammar schools, and then, in the post-Second World War world, the attempt to extend secondary education to all on comprehensive lines; the growth of further and adult education; the building up of public sector higher education.

The London County Council, even more than the London School Board, became a showcase for progressive policies – or rather, for the Labour party machine, perfected in the early 1930s by the then Mr Herbert Morrison. Political tension between County Hall on the south bank of the Thames, and Westminster on the north, continued with the more or less permanent exclusion of the Conservatives from positions of power in London.

The organisation of education in London came up for radical reconsideration again in 1960 when the Herbert Commission reported on the future of London's government and recommended the creation of a Greater London Council and an inner and outer ring of refurbished London boroughs. The Herbert Commission devised a method of splitting control of education between the GLC and the inner London boroughs on lines reminiscent of the abortive 1902 proposals. This scheme, however, aroused fierce opposition from the London education community and the vested interests centred on the old London County Council Education Committee; and also from the Ministry of Education, which resisted anything which threatened the integrity of the inner London area as a single education authority. When the LCC was abolished, therefore, a new, uniquely-constituted, Inner London Education Authority was created as a 'special committee' of the Greater London Council, with membership drawn from the GLC members representing inner London constituencies, augmented by thirteen members appointed by the inner London boroughs and the City of London.

In 1978 there was another inquiry, headed by Sir Frank

(later Lord) Marshall. This was set up by the Conservatives on the Greater London Council, to review the arrangements for the government of London, with a view to reform as and when the Conservatives achieved power at Westminster (which occurred the following year).

Marshall was a leading Conservative in local government, a former leader of Leeds City Council, and chairman of the Association of Municipal Corporations. He came down firmly in favour of preserving the structure of a unitary authority because of 'the essential need to maintain equity and evenness of standards of provision in the inner city areas' and the pattern of existing institutions which had grown up with 'little regard for borough boundaries'. He therefore formally recommended that education in London should be entrusted to the boroughs collectively – that is, through the formation of an Inner London Borough Statutory Joint Committee, under Schedule 1, Part 2, of the 1944 Education Act.

No action followed. After the General Election of 1979, however, a group of London MPs led by Mr Kenneth Baker, then MP for St Marylebone, joined in a straightforward proposal for the abolition of the ILEA and the transfer of powers of education to the inner boroughs.

The Baker report was a light-weight effort, but it gained significance because of the growing hostility between the central Government and the Inner London Education Authority which followed a left-wing coup which turned out the former Labour leader, Sir Ashley Bramall – the same coup displaced Mr Andrew Mackintosh as leader of the GLC and replaced him with Mr Ken Livingstone.

A review of Government policy, conducted by Lady Young, Minister of State at the DES (1981), once again considered breaking up the inner London area, but rejected it on pragmatic grounds. Lady Young restated the classic case for 'a single authority of adequate size and with adequate resources', while castigating the authority for its shortcomings and financial extravagance.

Both the GLC and the ILEA remained at loggerheads with the central Government, particularly in regard to expenditure policy. The central Government was determined to control local spending. A sequence of measures imposed penalties, in the form of reductions in Rate Support Grant, on high-spending local authorities of whom the ILEA was one. London ceased to receive any subsidy from the Rate Support Grant, but still persisted in spending more than the central Government approved. From 1984 onwards, the ILEA was 'rate-capped' and the Government insisted on budgets which began to fall in real terms, albeit slowly.

The 1981 review had reprieved the ILEA for a while, but only briefly because by this time the Conservative guns had been turned on to the Greater London Council, the abolition of which was promised by the Party's manifesto at the 1983 general election. If the GLC were abolished, the ILEA would be abolished too unless some other *ad hoc* solution were devised.

The ILEA fought a bruising campaign, with a high-level of parental support, and managed to convince Conservative as well as Labour MPs that it should be allowed to survive the demise of its parent body. At the last minute, Sir Keith Joseph, the Secretary of State for Education and Science, lined up behind a plan to turn the ILEA into a directly-elected, single-purpose education authority (the first since the abolition of the London School Board). This was duly enacted in 1985.

By now, however, the pace of the political battle had been stepped up and what had been legislated only in 1985 was scrapped in 1988. There was only time for one direct election to the ILEA before it received its quietus.

Educational standards and costs
The attack on education standards and high costs was linked in a single sentence in the Government discussion document published in advance of the Bill itself:

> 'there was severe criticism of the ILEA on the grounds of its educational performance despite levels of expenditure far in excess of any other LEA in the country'.

Some critics concentrated on London's examination record. A comparison of examination results by authority showed London near the bottom of the list, with 15.5 per cent of pupils getting five or more higher grade O-levels or CSE grade 1s compared with an all-England average of 23.7 per cent. It was a matter of continuing argument, however, how such statistics should be interpreted. It was beyond dispute that, if the *quality of the schools* was being considered rather than the actual performance of the pupils, the raw examination figures had to be adjusted to take account of social, economic and linguistic factors in the inner city.

Pupils obtaining five or more O-levels grades A–C and CSE grade 1	
	%
ILEA	15.5
Outer London Boroughs	24.4
Metropolitan Districts	20.6
English Counties	25.3
England	23.7

Source: DES: School leavers sample survey, averaged over academic years 1983–84, 1984–85 and 1985–86

On the basis of extensive research, Dr David Jeeson and Dr John Gray of Sheffield University produced their own league table of local authority performance, discounted for background environmental factors. This put London in 56th place out of 96 – 0.4 percentage points below par (represented in the table by West Sussex and Lincolnshire).

This conclusion seemed to be in line with the 1987 report prepared by Mr Eric Bolton, the senior chief HMI, based on inspectors' visits in the months before the preparation of the Education Reform Bill. He summed up in carefully balanced terms:

'Secondary education in the ILEA is generally rather poor though there are a few schools of high quality mainly in the voluntary sector. Of the 2500 lessons seen by HM inspectorate 60 per cent were judged to be satisfactory or better, including 20 per cent that were good; 40 per cent were unsatisfactory or poor . . . Pupils taking public examinations at 16 in the ILEA do less well in absolute terms than their counterparts from maintained schools in England as a whole; when the results are statistically adjusted for socio-economic factors the ILEA appears to perform up to expectations. . . .'

	Primary £	Secondary £
Costs per pupil		
ILEA	1 715.0	2 635.2
Outer London Boroughs	1 108.9	1 733.8
Metropolitan Districts	1 003.5	1 551.7
English Counties	926.4	1 454.9
England	1 008.7	1 563.1

Source: Education Statistics 1987–88 Estimates, CIPFA

As for costs, London consistently spent more than the sums which the Department of the Environment assessed to be necessary to provide a standard level of service – the so-called Grant Related Expenditure Assessments (GREs). There were perfectly respectable technical arguments with which to call the validity of the GREs in question. The ILEA believed they underestimated the real cost of meeting the concentration of social need in the capital. But London's high spending was also a matter of policy. London's political leaders rejected the central Government's priorities and deliberately maintained staffing and personnel policies – as, for example, in relation to the redeployment of staff, and the adjustment of staff numbers to pupil numbers in the face of falling pupil rolls – which kept unit costs far above those demanded by the Government.

The argument about costs, like the argument about the size of the ILEA and the merits or demerits of a single education authority for London, ultimately turned into a political struggle between the central Government and the largest and most conspicuous of recalcitrant local authorities. The leaders of the ILEA determined to defy the central Government. In so doing they encompassed their own destruction.

Development plans
How long it will take the new London education authorities to establish their own styles and policies, remains to be seen. The

Act itself set out what they had to do, and laid down the basic procedure which the DES then augments with detailed guidance.

By 28 February 1989 – that is within about seven months of the passing of the Act – the boroughs were required to submit development plans, following the format set out in the guidance issued by the DES in the early summer of 1988.

The task was formidable in the limited time, especially for those reluctant authorities which had been unwilling to make a start till the Act was in position. They had to begin by making plans for the setting up of an education committee and a senior staff structure for the education department.

Parts of the development plan were routine but nevertheless time-consuming. A lot of basic reference material – about schools and other property which the new authority did or did not wish to take over – was required, along with the detailed demographic statistics and the five-year projections needed to relate the lists of 'inherited' schools to the expected child populations. The guidance document drew special attention to the need to review provision for the 16–19 age-range in schools and colleges. The ILEA had already spent many months in negotiations and consultations at the divisional level on plans for tertiary institutions which had been held up by the Secretary of State. Rationalisation was already urgent by the time the Bill became an Act.

The plan also had to cover the national curriculum and the authority's own curriculum policy; policy for special needs (hitherto developed on an ILEA-wide basis); and policy for ethnic minorities, adult education, in-service training, the careers service, the youth service, the local inspectorate, school meals and school transport.

Behind the list of topics were the technical and policy questions arising from the break up of a unitary system and its replacement by a dozen or so separate systems. The memorandum of guidance referred to this on the second page. Improvements in the performance and accountability of the education service were 'urgently needed', which prompted the suggested possibility that some authorities might establish 'arrangements for cooperation'. These, the Secretary of State thought, 'are likely to be most effective where they operate on a voluntary basis rather than under the formal provisions for a joint education committee under . . . the Education Act 1944'.

Free trade between the inner London authorities for school and college admissions could be seen as an essential prerequisite of making the new, decentralised, London systems work. Much effort would be needed to prevent unnecessary damage to the familiar roll-call of London-wide services (adult education, the careers service, special needs, the youth service, music . . .), but the logic of the break-up certainly implied that not all of these activities would continue to be supported at the former level. That represented the price the authors of the Bill were prepared to pay to get rid of the ILEA. In many of these areas, the development plans could only aim at keeping the damage to a minimum.

Adult education emerged during the debates on the Bill as one of the parts of the London education service which was most vulnerable in the handover to the boroughs. Not only were the geographical factors such as to make nonsense of borough boundaries, but the ILEA spent more than three times as much on this activity as the Rate Support Grant allowed – £42 million compared with £13 million. So at the same time as wrestling with the structural difficulties of splitting up a unitary system, the boroughs would have to make massive cuts – because London had generated more demand than the Rate Support Grant was geared to recognise.

Finance

It was made clear in the DES guidance that the new education authorities were to be expected to reduce spending to the levels provided for in the Rate Support Grant. If they failed to do so, they would have to find the additional cost from their own resources (i.e. the community charge) with the high rate of gearing which that implied.

The transition is to be eased by 'safety net' arrangements which mean the inner boroughs have till 1994–95 to get control of their finances. In the case of those boroughs which are, themselves, already rate-capped, the cuts in education have to be managed alongside cuts in all other services.

Action

It is difficult to forecast the impact of London reorganisation on the schools, the staff and governing bodies, except in terms of a catalogue of potential disasters in the short term, followed, at best, by a period of consolidation.

Each school has had to recruit a new governing body, or persuade the existing governors to offer themselves for election or appointment if eligible. It is difficult to imagine that the administrative changes can be accomplished without some dislocation and delay – in appointments, in handling correspondence and queries, in taking decisions. The changes in London provide a counterpoint to other changes required by other sections of the Act – local financial management, which in London is to be brought in between 1991 and 1994; the increased powers of governors over appointments; the national curriculum; open enrolment.

The impact of reorganisation and local management of schools on the advisory services has interrupted the school improvement plans at primary and secondary level already begun by the ILEA since the Hargreaves Inquiry into secondary education (1984) and the Thomas Report on primary schools (1985) are to be implemented. The difficulties of maintaining continuity (notwithstanding Section 195) promise to be real enough.

Continuity may now be in conflict with the legitimate wishes of newly created education authorities to exercise the powers and responsibilities given to them by the Act. Each of the new authorities has to prepare its own statement of curriculum policy, and seek to build up a sense of common purpose behind its own interpretation of the national curriculum. Each will pick over the ILEA policies on multicultural education and equal opportunities. Each will engage in its own debates on racism and ethnic issues.

Parents are promised a time of confusion and uncertainty which could reinforce the modest trend towards independent schooling. Where the local education authority is clearly competent, the transition is likely to be managed without any serious disruption, though this depends on how deep the financial cuts go and how they impact upon the teachers and their unions.

Where the local authority is weak and incompetent, parents may be more disposed to investigate the possibilities of grant-maintained status if the potential leaders for such a scheme present themselves.

8

Miscellaneous Provisions

City Technology Colleges

Section 105 gives a legal basis for the Secretary of State to enter into agreements with sponsors for the creation of two new types of independent schools, to be known as city technology colleges and city colleges for the technology of the arts. Section 105(2) lists the characteristics of such colleges: they must be situated in an urban area and provide education for pupils of different abilities in the 11–18 age range, drawn from the area where the school is situated. In the case of the city technology colleges, they must have 'a broad curriculum with an emphasis on science and technology'. The 'city colleges for the technology of the arts' must have 'a broad curriculum with an emphasis on technology in its application to the performing and creative arts'.

The Secretary of State is empowered to make grants and capital payments to such schools, which are to make no charge for admission (Section 105(3)). The section also lays down rules to be followed concerning the repayment of grants made by the Secretary of State in the event of the discontinuance of a city technology college or the termination of the agreement under which it was set up.

The introduction of this section into the Bill was to encourage the industrial and commercial sponsors on whom the Secretary of State depended for the creation of the city technology colleges. Part of the strategy of the scheme, announced in the summer of 1987, was to raise from industry a substantial sum for each of the twenty planned CTCs, as an earnest of continuing support. Although the powers of the Secretary of State under existing legislation covered the making of grants to private educational institutions such as CTCs, it was felt that statutory backing would give businessmen a greater sense of security in supporting a controversial educational initiative.

CTCs are independent schools. In curriculum terms they are bound by their agreement with the Secretary of State rather than by the terms of the national curriculum, but in practice they are likely to meet all or most of its requirements.

The first CTC opened at Kingshurst, Solihull, in September 1988. Colleges at Nottingham and Middlesbrough opened in September 1989. By September 1991, thirteen colleges were in operation – the three already mentioned plus colleges at Croydon, Dartford, Gateshead, Bradford, Selhurst, Lewisham, London Docklands, Corby, Telford and Wandsworth.

Early indications were that the colleges would take advantage of their independence to offer premium terms to teachers in the attempt to assemble high-grade staff, many of them in shortage subjects. Plans also showed a readiness to make the students work longer hours than in most maintained schools and combine academic study with work experience.

The refusal of some inner-city local authorities to make redundant schools and sites available, delayed progress – as did the hesitation of some well-known companies which were unwilling to become involved in projects which were resolutely opposed by the local authorities. In the event, funds subscribed from industry formed a smaller fraction of the capital costs of some of the early projects than had originally been hoped, with a correspondingly greater contribution from the DES in the form of capital grants (estimated at £9.05 million in the case of the Nottingham CTC). By 1989, some £43.2 million had been raised from industry and commerce for projected CTCs.

A proposal in the summer of 1988, put forward by a group of entertainment entrepreneurs, envisaged the formation of a private college on lines similar to the CTCs but dedicated to aspects of the performing arts – music, drama and dance.

This led to a late amendment to the original draft of the Bill which extended the definition of city technology colleges to take in 'colleges for the technology of the arts'. The terminology reflects the attempt to exploit the potential generosity of the popular music industry without appearing to depart entirely from the original concept of the CTCs, which was tied up with applied science and technology, and in particular with electronics and information technology.

The arts – performing and creative – were, therefore, to be admitted in order to respond to the initiative of Mr Richard Branson, the founder of Virgin Records, and a brilliant entrepreneur in the modern mould. But, to preserve the twenty-first-century, hi-tech basis of an initiative which closely reflected Mr Kenneth Baker's own romantic attachment to 'new' technology, the performing and creative arts had to be brought in by a technological back-door – through the electronics associated with the modern recording studio and music theatre. What became the Selhurst City College for Technology of the Arts is the first to specialise in the technology of the performing arts, with sponsorship from the electronic music industry.

Time will tell how closely the 'technology of the arts' colleges are held to their statutory obligations. There is clearly a role in big cities for 'magnet' schools specialising in the performing arts, and offering students high standards in music and dance, in particular. These colleges are meant to do more than this. The rubric should ensure that the college (or colleges) provide a broad curriculum and teach potential performers and creators about the mechanics of their art form. It may ensure that those whose talent fails to blossom in performance or in creativity have a sound education in science and technology, as well as their initiation into the arts, to fall back on.

Charges in maintained schools

The Education Reform Act provided the opportunity in Sections 106–111 to redefine 'free education' and clarify the powers and duties of local education authorities with regard to charges for services.

Section 106(1) prohibits the making of any charge for admission to any maintained schools. It goes on in subsection (2) to qualify this, by stating that no charge may be made for any education provided at any maintained school during school hours, except for 'individual tuition in playing a musical instrument' (subsection (3)). No charge can be made for any tuition if this is required as part of the syllabus for a prescribed public examination (subsection (4)).

The Section goes on to prohibit charges for examination fees, books and materials or transport to a public examination or to engage in a recognised part of the school course. Charges can, however, be levied for board and lodging on a residential trip.

A related section (118) makes clear that the prohibition of charging for admission and for most mainline activities should not 'be read as prohibiting or in any way restricting or regulating any request . . . by . . . the governing body . . . for voluntary contributions for the benefit of the school or any of its activities'.

Such a request may only be made, however, if 'it is clear from the terms in which it is made that (*a*) there is no obligation to make any contribution and (*b*) that registered pupils at the school will not be treated differently' if their parents do or do not contribute.

The background thinking behind these sections was set out in the consultative document issued in October 1987. In the four decades since the passing of the 1944 Education Act, local education authority practices on charging for 'extras' had begun to diverge. A case brought by a parent against the Hereford and Worcester education authority in 1981, over charges made for instrumental music tuition, caused section 61 of the 1944 Act to be construed in the High Court. Mr Justice Forbes favoured a wide interpretation of the section, requiring all activities coming within the school curriculum to be free.

In the context of tight curbs on spending, such an interpretation was more likely to cause local authorities to take instrumental tuition out of the curriculum than to lead them to extend the range of free provision. The DES reaction was to look for a form of words which would restore the status quo as it had been believed to exist before the Hereford and Worcester case came to court.

The form of words eventually chosen explicitly permits charging for individual instrumental tuition and for board and lodging in connection (for example) with field trips. But neither exception would apply if the activity in question were required for a prescribed public examination.

The sections go into further detail over such matters as educational activities which extend beyond 'school hours', the recovery of examination fees from the parents of pupils who fail to attend, and 'optional extras'.

One consequence of the new legislation is that every body of school governors and every local education authority must now have a 'charging policy' (Section 110). The new sections do not force local authorities or school governors to charge for any services hitherto provided free, if these services fall within the legal powers of the authority. But, for the purpose of the Rate Support Grant the provisions of these sections will form the basis of the Government's calculations of what local authorities need to spend.

No Sections of the Act caused more confusion at the level of the individual school than those on charging. In an attempt to clarify matters, the DES issued Circular 2/89 in January 1989 which was widely thought to have added to the general uncertainty. The effect of the change in the law was to reduce the number of school visits including cultural activities such as theatre matinées. Visits to the theatre have to be paid for by the school from its budget share if they are essential for a recognised course. If regarded as an 'optional extra', any charge must be voluntary and may not include any element of subsidy for children whose parents cannot or will not pay. No activity can be an 'optional extra' if it takes place during school hours.

The Circular offered guidance on how schools might go about soliciting voluntary gifts, the continuing importance of which the Act had stressed in Section 118. This emphasised that any request for voluntary contributions must make it quite clear to parents that they were under no obligation to contribute – i.e. that voluntary really means voluntary. And secondly, the request must explain that 'the registered pupils at a school will not be treated differently according to whether or not their parents have made any contribution in response to the request'. This applies to fundraising for any specific school activity, whether during or outside school hours. Voluntary contributions can be solicited for school funds generally, and in particular circumstances school funds can be used to subsidise activities. Charges for board and lodging on residential visits have to be remitted for children whose parents are on income support or family credit.

An apparent loop-hole was opened up in paragraph 18 of the Circular, headed 'Activities arranged during school hours by a third party'. This dealt with occasions when 'an organisation other than the local authority or governing body' arranges some activity or trip during school hours and parents ask for leave of absence for their children to take part. 'Under Section 118(4) the third party would be able to levy charges direct on the parents' of those taking part. The local authority and governing body would stand aside and it would be 'for parents and any staff members released for the activity to satisfy themselves about the adequacy of the arrangements made by the third party to secure the safety and welfare of the children . . . '

The first reaction to the new rules on charging on the part of schools and governing bodies was one of caution. Few schools or authorities had settled their charging policies by April 1, 1989 when these Sections of the Act came into force. Schools were feeling their way. The DES Circular itself seemed more than usually anxious to make clear the tentative nature of its advice.

Power to determine times of school sessions

Governing bodies are given the power to decide on the length of the school day and how this should be organised. Section 115 amends the Education (No.2) Act 1986 and states that the Articles of Government of every county, Controlled and maintained special school should provide for this as one of the governors' responsibilities. The local authority retains the duty to fix the school terms.

Various conditions are attached to this power. To make a change in the school day, the governors have to consult the local authority and include notice of any proposed change (with the local authority's comments) in the annual report to parents. They have to give parents an opportunity to comment. They must consider any views which are forthcoming. A change can only be made at the beginning of a school year. Parents must be given three months notice of any change.

The increased flexibility which this will bring will increase the ability of the school to make its own response to the demands of the national curriculum. Some schools will certainly respond to the pressure on the timetable by extending the school day. This is particularly likely for pupils in the fourth and fifth years of the secondary school.

Education Assets Board

The Act provides for a change of ownership and control for large numbers of educational institutions – most notably those polytechnics and higher education colleges which are removed from the local authority sector and brought under the Polytechnics and Colleges Funding Council, and those county schools which acquire grant-maintained school status.

Section 197 sets up an Education Assets Board to perform various technical services on behalf of the Secretary of State in connection with the transfer of assets as a result of the changes in ownership and control. The White Paper on *Higher Education: Meeting the Challenge* (1987) foreshadowed the creation of this body, its main task being to 'resolve any difficulties in the apportionment of assets to transferred institutions and to assist them to make arrangements as quickly as possible for the holding of their own assets'. It was subsequently decided to extend the functions of the Assets Board to cover the transfer of property and assets of schools which cease to be maintained by local authorities after 'opting out'.

The detailed duties of the Board are set out in Section 198 and Schedules 8 and 10 to the Act. These include sorting out, identifying and apportioning property rights and liabilities, and determining payments due to former governing bodies and local authorities, where appropriate.

Unrecognised degrees

The Education Reform Act tackles the long-term nuisance of bogus degrees in Sections 214–217.

The Act defines certain 'recognised awards' – those made by chartered universities or bodies authorised by Parliament to award degrees, and 'such other awards as the Secretary of State may by order designate' (Section 214(2)).

It becomes a criminal offence to sell unrecognised degrees or anything else which is alleged to confer the right to the title of bachelor, master or doctor or may be reasonably taken to be a degree (Section 214(1)).

To prove an offence it has to be shown that an award was granted or offered or that an invitation relating to an award was issued. It is also necessary to show that the documents relating to the award are issued from an address in the United Kingdom.

Section 214(5) and (6) protects the British agents of foreign institutions offering degrees in the United Kingdom. These are not affected by the legislation, provided they are properly authorised by foreign institutions and make it clear in all their dealings with the public that the awards or degrees which they are offering are granted by a foreign institution.

Enforcement is entrusted to the local Weights and Measures Officer, whose extensive powers of entry and search are set out in Section 215.

The scandal of the bogus degree mills had long been a disgrace which the Department of Education and Science had failed to deal with. One reason for the hesitation was an uncertainty about the amount of supervision which would be needed to stamp it out. The escape clauses for foreign institutions show how difficult it is likely to prove in practice to put an end to this form of confidence trickery.

A number of United States institutions market unaccredited degrees in Britain offering to give academic recognition to experience gained in the practice of business or administration. The DES has no way of distinguishing between genuine practitioners in 'experiential learning' and sharks selling bogus American certificates. Nor does it intend to get into the business of accrediting overseas degrees. But without a control on the import of 'unrecognised degrees' these sections are of limited use.

Extension of functions of the Audit Commission

Section 220 has the effect of extending the remit of the Audit Commission for Local Authorities in England and Wales to enable it to continue to be concerned with the 'economy, efficiency and effectiveness' in the management or operations of the Polytechnics and Colleges Funding Council, the higher education corporations and grant-maintained schools.

Application of Employment law

Section 222 is a catch-all clause which gives the Secretary of State overriding power, by Order, to 'make such modifications in any enactment relating to employment . . . as he considers necessary or expedient in consequence of the operation of any of the provisions of the Act' relating to changes in employment resulting from local school management and financial delegation, and the delegation of powers to FE college governors. Such modifications as the Secretary of State might make under this Section would be to any enactment:

'(a) conferring powers or imposing duties on employers.

'(b) conferring rights on employees; or

'(c) otherwise regulating the relations between employers and employees.'

This Section, and the sweeping powers it confers on the Secretary of State, came in for much comment in debates on the Bill in Parliament and outside. The Section stems from the delegation of staff management functions to further education colleges and schools, required by Sections 33–47 and 139–149. Under such schemes, the employer remains the local authority, but responsibility for hiring and firing is devolved to the board of governors of the school or college. The powers which the Secretary of State is taking are deemed necessary to deal with complications which arise from employment legislation designed for different circumstances.

In expounding the Bill, the DES gave as an example the situation which might arise if the governing body of a county school with financial delegation required the local authority to give notice of dismissal to an employee who worked for the school. The passage of Section 222 would enable the Secretary of State to amend the rules so as to make the governing body (rather than the local authority) defend the action if challenged in an Industrial Tribunal. This would involve altering the statutory provisions concerning unfair dismissal in Part V of the Employment Protection (Consolidation) Act 1978. This is only one example of the responsibilities which have to be transferred to the governors by modifying the previous enactment.

Services for British schools in Europe

Section 226 was added at a late stage during the passage of the Bill through the House of Lords, on the initiative of Lady Young, a former DES Minister of State. Its aim was to help British schools in Continental countries of the European Community which provide education on curricular lines similar to those of maintained schools in England and Wales.

A duty is imposed on the Secretary of State by Section 226(2) to provide such schools with regular information on educational developments in England and Wales. And in addition, he must respond to a request from such schools for inspection from time to time, charging the schools the full cost.

This was unwelcome to the DES, which has always regarded the existence of private British schools abroad as none of its business, though ex-HMIs have provided various services to these schools in the past. It is not clear what the effect of the new Section will be. The Government accepted it, reluctantly, because it did not seem likely to add up to any significant change. Overseas inspections are costly, and if the Secretary of State charges the full cost of any service of this kind, the British school abroad will have to foot a large bill.

The Section applies only to the British independent sector in Europe, and not to H.M. Forces schools.

9

School Governors' Powers and Duties

School governors emerge from the Education Reform Act with much-enhanced powers and more demanding duties. It is to the school governors that the Act delivers many of the functions hitherto performed by local education authorities. The same Act which gives the Secretary of State a much stronger strategic grip on the curriculum and on higher education, devolves more of the tactical decision-making to the governors, who represent lay authority at the level of the individual school and college site.

Not every education system finds it necessary to have school governors – the Scots, for example, have managed to run a democratic education system without this degree of decentralised control. An attempt to assemble Scottish support for the introduction of this 'English' device, as a preliminary for the introduction of some Scottish equivalent to grant-maintained schools, produced a hostile reaction which forced Scottish Office ministers to beat a retreat.[1]

Governors have evolved in England and Wales over many generations. 'Governors' and 'managers' were running schools long before the first elected school boards came into existence after 1870. In the early nomenclature, secondary schools had governors and elementary schools (and, later, primary schools) had managers – a form of class distinction which survived until the 1980 Education Act. The governors and managers of pre-1870 schools had the main responsibility for making and keeping them viable. Many of these schools survived the 1870 Education Act as voluntary schools.

After 1870, school managers passed into the public sector –

the London School Board, for instance, appointed some 3000 managers for its elementary schools:

> 'They selected and appointed heads . . . investigated complaints . . . They had to appoint a health sub-committee . . . to look after the "dull and delicate". Each year they had to report on the health of the children, the curriculum, the state and use of libraries, the "extra-scholastic" efforts of the school, the incidence of poverty and destitution and any special plans for interesting parents in the work of the schools.'[2]

From 1889 onwards every group of managers had 'as far as possible' to include two parents or ex-parents of elementary school children.

It is easy to see, therefore, how the idea that every school should have its own local board of management became part of the conventional wisdom. In the voluntary and the independent sector, governors and managers were a necessary part of the system, small groups of men and women who came together to 'provide' a school and keep it going. Given the large numbers of voluntary schools and the high prestige of the independent schools, it is not surprising that the idea was taken over into the public system.

When the architects of the 1944 Education Act sought to devise legal structures to accommodate the religious compromise which gave a new deal to the Church schools, they set out in Sections 17–22 of the Act a statutory basis for governors' activities. These Sections included the arrangements for the sharing of power in voluntary schools between representatives of the local education authority and the voluntary body concerned. In voluntary Controlled schools, the (usually) Church authorities, appointed a third of the members, the local authority nominees being in a clear majority. In voluntary Aided and Special Agreement schools, the local authority would have only one-third of the seats and the Church authorities, the 'foundation', would have the majority vote.

As to the powers of governors under the 1944 Act, in county schools these varied from one local authority to another. Some authorities, like Manchester, went against the spirit of the Act by grouping schools together and entrusting the function of management to a sub-committee of the education committee. Governors in country areas tended to have more responsibility and influence – in regard, for instance, to appointments – than governing and managing bodies in towns. There was some truth in the caricature of the governors as a 'backing group' which performed ceremonial duties at speech days and other school functions but which had few serious tasks to perform on a day-to-day basis. Even so, the governors and managers could find themselves with a real job to do in times of crisis – when a pupil or a teacher might have to be suspended, or the future of the school itself was under discussion.

During the 1970s attitudes began to change. There was a disposition to challenge the notion that governors should be restricted to a mainly decorative role. By origin, governors had been 'providers' organisations'. As such they had been overtaken by events and by the march of bureaucracy. Could they be turned into combined 'consumers' and providers' organisations', representing the users and the local community to the local authority, rather than the other way round?

Some local authorities – Sheffield was a notable example – began to look for ways of extending the role and increasing the representative character of governing bodies. There was a rising tide of consumerism which encouraged the idea of more direct participation by parents. By the time of the Callaghan Ruskin College speech in 1976, the Labour Government had already set up the Taylor Committee to review the arrangements for the government of maintained schools, including the composition and the function of governing bodies and their relationships with teachers, parents and the community at large.

The report, which appeared in 1977, recommended some strengthening of the powers of Governors and a radical change in the composition of governing bodies, with membership shared equally between local authority representatives, teachers, the parents and the local community.[3]

It got a mixed reception. Some of the teachers' unions were highly sceptical – Mr Fred Jarvis, the general secretary of the NUT, branded it a 'busy-bodies' charter'. The scepticism was not wholly restricted to the teachers. The governors' power over money was in no way increased and, while the Taylor Report advocated more say for the governors in setting the aims of a school in its curriculum and ethos, there was ample room for conflict among the separate groups which would make up each governing body. The local education authorities disliked it as much as the teachers.

Labour attempts to put parts of the Taylor Report into law in 1979 were overtaken by a general election, but in 1980 the incoming Conservatives introduced a Bill which made a start on the reform of governing bodies. It required at least two elected parent-governors in county and voluntary Controlled schools, one or two elected teacher-governors and the head (if so desiring) to be included on governing bodies. It also restricted the grouping of schools under a single board of governors by making such schemes subject to direct DES approval. It did little to extend the powers of governors, but it gave modest recognition to the parents' and teachers' interest – a minimum response, perhaps, but a stepping stone on the way to more radical measures later on.

Modest as the changes were, they introduced elected parent-governors to many schools which had never before had them. Other parts of the 1980 Act reflected the continuing interest in making local education authorities and schools more responsible, by requiring much more information on each school and on admissions policies to be published, and by giving parents the right to send their children across borough or county boundaries to the school of their choice.

Sir Keith Joseph's incumbency at the DES brought a more aggressive approach to consumer questions in education, both in respect of the empowering of individual parents by giving them choice, and in the matter of their representation on governing bodies. In 1984 Sir Keith issued a Green Paper[4] which went a long way beyond anything put forward in the Taylor Report. It proposed that there should be many more elected parent-governors, giving them an absolute majority in county schools and enlarged representation in voluntary Controlled schools. With this increase in parent power went increased powers for the reconstituted governing bodies – powers which were defined in detail in the Green Paper because, in the Government's view, the situation which had evolved from custom and practice since 1944 was 'confusing, unsatisfactory for parents and teachers, and harmful to good education'.

The Green Paper set out to define the respective responsibilities of the local education authority, the governors and the headteacher as a preliminary to setting these down in legislation. In so doing, it ran the risk of destroying fragile working relationships, but the risk was thought to be necessary as a means of creating a clearly defined territory for governors.

The proposal that parents should elect the majority of seats on governing bodies from among their own number was rejected by most of those consulted by the DES in the wake of the Green Paper. Most significantly, it was rejected by the organised parents' groups and by the National Association of Governors and Managers. The effect of the Green Paper proposals was to consolidate support behind the Taylor proposals. Even those who had originally had doubts about the quadripartite split recommended by Taylor now seemed to see this as the ideal formula.

As with other aspects of educational reform in the 1980s, there have been two separate and distinct bites at this particular cherry. The first instalment came with Sir Keith Joseph's 1986 Education (No. 2) Act; the second with Mr Kenneth Baker's 1988 Education Reform Act.

The 1986 Act revised the composition of governing bodies and extended their powers over the curriculum and the conduct of the school. The 1988 Act left the composition of school governing bodies unchanged, but revised the rules about the curriculum, appointments and school management in the course of legislation on the national curriculum and local financial delegation.

For the purpose of this chapter, the Education (No. 2) Act is the master document so far as school governing bodies are concerned. But the 1988 Education Reform Act modified the 1986 provisions by greatly increasing the responsibilities of governors and the range of tasks entrusted to them. The two Acts have to be read together with the 1944 Education Act, therefore, by anyone who wants to understand the position which governing bodies now occupy in the education systems of England and Wales.

Composition of governing bodies

The formula for the composition of school governing bodies adopted in response to the consultations which followed Sir Keith Joseph's 1984 Green Paper is set out in Sections 1–4 of the 1986 Act.

For county, voluntary Controlled, and maintained special schools:

Less than 100 pupils:
   2 parents
   2 LEA-appointed
   1 teacher
   1 head (unless he chooses not to be a governor)
   and *either*
   2 foundation governors (in the case of a voluntary school)
   and 1 co-opted
   or
   3 co-opted

100–299 pupils:
   3 parents
   3 LEA-appointed
   1 teacher
   1 head (unless he chooses not to be a governor)
   and *either*
   3 foundation governors
   and 1 co-opted
   or
   4 co-opted

300–599 pupils:
   4 parents
   4 LEA-appointed
   2 teachers
   1 head (unless he chooses not to be a governor)
   and *either*
   4 foundation governors
   and 1 co-opted
   or
   5 co-opted

More than 600 pupils:
  5 parents
  5 LEA-appointed
  2 teachers
  1 head (unless he chooses not to be a governor)
  and *either*
  4 foundation
  and 2 co-opted
  or
  6 co-opted

Different rules apply to voluntary Aided and Special Agreement schools. For such schools there must be:

  1 LEA-appointed
  1 (at least) parent
  1 or 2 teachers (depending on whether there are more or fewer than 300 pupils)
  1 head (unless he chooses not to be a governor)

plus enough foundation governors to ensure they outnumber the rest by two in a governing body of less than eighteen and three in the case of a larger body. One of the foundation governors must also be a parent. In the case of primary schools serving an area in which there is a minor local authority, the minor authority can appoint one governor.

Instruments and Articles of Government
For every county, voluntary and maintained special school there has to be

(*a*) an instrument providing for the constitution of a governing body . . . (to be known as the Instrument of Government)
(*b*) an instrument in accordance with which the school is to be conducted . . . (to be known as the Articles of Government) (DES Circular 7/87[5]).

Instrument of Government
In setting out the *constitution* of a governing body, this document lays down who are to be the members: the various categories from which they are to be drawn, and in what numbers. It

includes rules about the holding of meetings, quorums, the election of a chairman, the attendance of members and relations with the business community.

All governors (except the headteachers) hold office for a four-year term. Teacher-governors automatically cease to hold office if they leave the staff.

Local education authorities do not have to prepare a separate Instrument for every school. As the DES guidance puts it in Circular 7/87:

> 'block instruments and articles may be made, provided each indicates clearly both the names of the schools to which it applies and any distinctive provisions for individual schools.'

It is still possible under the law to group several schools under a single governing body, but 'the presumption is that every school will have its own individual governing body' unless an authority can satisfy the Secretary of State that there are very strong reasons to regard the interdependence of several schools as of over-riding importance. No one may be on more than four maintained school governing bodies.

Articles of Government

These set out the *governors' responsibilities* for the running of the school, and relate these responsibilities to the functions and duties of the local education authority and the headteacher.

Conduct of the school

The governors have overall responsibility for the 'conduct of the school', which is said to be 'under the direction' of the governors (Education (No. 2) Act, Section 16(1)). Under this heading come all the intangible considerations which go to define the ethos of a school. Clearly, many of these are outside the immediate control of the governors and rest with the head, who is charged with the 'determination and organisation of the secular curriculum' (Section 18(5)).

It is no part of the Education Reform Act to take away the

powers of management vested in the head – rather, the opposite is true – but it is obvious that there is scope for an over-zealous governing body to get at cross-purposes with an over-zealous head. The secret of the successful school will, as always, lie in the effective cooperation between the professional leadership (the head and his/her staff), the lay government (the governors) and the local authority and its advisers. The Articles of Government purport to clarify this relationship, but often this clarification takes the form of more ambiguities and blurred distinctions. The power of the governors in relation to the ethos of the school will rest in their ability to call for reports and explanations – the ability to make clear their approval and their criticisms of particular aspects of the school, as they are aware of its reputation and character. Whether this power is enough to justify the description of the governors as the body under whose direction the school operates, is a moot point.

For much of the time the governors' powers will resemble those ascribed by Bagehot to the monarch under the British Constitution: they can advise, warn and demand to be informed. They have considerable disciplinary powers available to them in extreme circumstances (see below) and if they choose to exert strong pressure they can make the position of the head untenable. By the same token, their strong support can sustain a head through a period of difficulty.

Curriculum

The enactment of the National Curriculum sections of the 1988 Act had the effect of amending parts of the 1986 Act before they had even been brought into operation. Thus, Section 1(1) makes it the unequivocal duty of the governing body (and of the local authority and the headteacher) to see that the national curriculum is implemented, along with the legal requirements for religious education.

The national curriculum is, however, only the starting point. Each local authority and school has to put its own gloss on it. The local education authority must review its policy on curricular matters and prepare its own statement of policy. School governors must consider this alongside the national curriculum and the various Orders which incorporate it. It is then for the school governors to prepare their own policy document on the curriculum (Education (No. 2) Act, Section 18). The governors' power to 'modify' the local authority policy does not mean they can ignore it or reject it out of hand, but it does mean they can vary it in important matters of detail and emphasis. The law requires the governors to consult with the head and to 'have regard to' any representations made to them by the local community. In particular, there is an obligation on the governors to consult the chief officer of police in their area, and to consult the local authority on any points in their policy statement which cut across that of the local authority.

Both the governors' curriculum policy document and the local authority's must be compatible with the national curriculum, which is binding on all the partners: the local authority, the governors and the headteacher.

Only time will tell how significant the role of the local authority and the governors will be in tailoring the national curriculum to local needs. If local authorities, which retain some responsibility for the allocation of resources, have strong social or political aims which they wish to impress upon the schools they will still have the opportunity to make their views well known. But the schools will not be forced to toe the authority's line so long as they remain firmly within the terms of the national curriculum. Their duty is to follow the national curriculum, in the light of the local authority's policy, *as modified* by the governing body.

In many schools it will fall to the head to draw up the draft policy statement on the curriculum for the governors, in the light of their own discussions and the head's intended interpretation of the national curriculum.

The governors' legal responsibilities in regard to the curriculum mean that they will expect to examine carefully any draft which is put before them and to get a full explanation from the professionals on any point which they wish to pursue. The law would certainly permit them to go a long way beyond this and prepare a draft of their own. In practice, governors will generally be reluctant to attempt this, even when they are not wholly satisfied with what the head offers them, because their resources in time, expertise and secretarial assistance will be limited; and if there are any governors among them who do happen to have had past professional experience of running a school, they will be rightly reluctant to act in any way which might seem to undermine the head.

If they are unlikely to take over the task themselves, it does not mean that they will not expect to influence the document and put their own stamp on it. The governors' role in regard to the curriculum will depend very much on local circumstances, on the kind of people on the governing body, and on the skill and tact of the headteacher. In most places it will be the head who provides the main input and therefore gets the outcome which he or she wants.

The requirement to consult the local police chief was a bizarre late addition to the 1986 Bill in the House of Lords. Hostility between the police and teachers and youth leaders in inner-city areas was a reflection of bad relations between the police and young people. Such bad relations are inevitable in areas with high rates for petty crime and drug offences, where most of the offenders are young people.

Ill-considered small-scale attempts by some sections of the Inner London Teachers Association – the local branch of the National Union of Teachers – to institutionalise this hostility by making strict rules to restrict police access to the schools, received exaggerated publicity. This reinforced right-wing fears that the schools were breeding-grounds for anti-police sentiment, run by teachers who were left-wing activists. In truth, the schools which sought to keep the police at arms length were heavily outnumbered by others where good relationships were maintained. But this said, it was clear that there was a strong minority opinion among young teachers which was hostile to the police.

The peers who introduced the amendment which has brought the chief of police into consultation on the curriculum, simply seized the opportunity which the Bill offered, to draw attention to what they saw as the schools' duty to preach law and order and cooperation with authority. They were, doubtless, less concerned with the mechanism of curriculum-building, than with sending a signal to the schools to teach children the difference between right and wrong, and to cooperate with the police in crime prevention.

Exactly how governing bodies and police officers will carry out the consultation which is now legally required of them remains to be seen. It is extremely unlikely that individual police officers will have the time or the inclination to wade through the documentation on the curriculum which would be necessary if serious consultation were to take place. Nor is it likely that, whatever the police chief's views, they will be formulated in a way which fits into a general discussion of the curriculum. But the Act does provide the police with leverage for securing the schools' cooperation in the development and use of teaching materials about crime, its prevention, and the obligations of good citizenship. Schools, themselves, will be that much more likely to include such teaching in their programmes – and to invite the police to take part – because of the statutory requirement.

Sex education

On sex education, the 1986 Act, Section 18(2), gave governors a particular role to play. This is restated in the Education Reform Act 1988 and applied to grant-maintained schools. It is up to the governors to decide whether or not any sex education should be included in the curriculum, and to 'make and keep up to date' a written statement of their policy on the content and organisation of such teaching, if they decide that sex education should be given. There is another legal requirement in the same Act (Section 46) which stipulates that, if sex education is provided, it must be given 'in such a manner as to encourage . . . pupils to have due regard to moral considerations and the value of family life'.

Like the requirement to consult the police on the curriculum, the sex education provisions of the 1986 Act were added in the House of Lords at a late stage in the Bill's parliamentary progress, when a group of peers saw an opportunity to strike a blow against permissiveness. The effect of the specific references to sex education was modified by Section 18(6)(c) of the 1986 Act, which made it legal to teach anything required by a syllabus for a course leading to a public examination, thereby avoiding a situation in which a govenors' ban on sex education might inhibit biology teaching.

Here again, the Education Reform Act 1988 may further modify the 1986 rules – in this case, to curb the governors' discretion rather than to extend it. The National Curriculum, introduced under Sections 1–3 of the 1988 Act, keys into the examinations of the General Certificate of Secondary Education. This being so, it might be argued that programmes of study introduced by Order for the national curriculum in science are part of a course leading to a public examination. The original proposals put forward by the Secretary of State's working group would require all pupils in the last two years to study the technology and practice of contraception as part of a balanced science course, but this was omitted from the National Curriculum Council's recommendations.

This is, of course, no more than a particular example of the extent to which the national curriculum is limiting schools' discretion, at the same time that other parts of the legislation are seeking to extend the decision-making powers of the governors.

Governors also have to take account of Section 28 of the Local Government Act 1988, which forbids local authorities to:

(*a*) Intentionally promote homosexuality or publish material with the intention of promoting homosexuality;
(*b*) promote the teaching in any maintained school for the acceptability of homosexuality as a pretended family relationship.

Length of the school day
Governors' powers over the conduct of the school were significantly extended by Section 115, which was added to the original Bill by a Government amendment during its passage through Parliament. This gives governing bodies the responsibility for fixing the times of school sessions. Within school terms, which the local authority continues to determine, governors of county, Controlled and maintained special schools can now decide how many hours a day the school is to be open and how the sessions are to be organised. This discretion is subject to various condi-

tions, aimed at discouraging governing bodies from being unduly eccentric, enabling the local education authority to advise and warn, and ensuring that parents have plenty of notice of a change and opportunity to make their opinions known.

This additional power is going to be important in two respects. First, it enables schools to experiment with the so-called 'continental day' in which school starts and finishes earlier, with reduced time for breaks at mid-day. Such arrangements may be convenient in some localities. Some schools may favour them because they may make it easier to arrange after-school activities. Others may see ways of saving on heating and lighting. After financial delegation, any such savings would accrue to the school.

Second, this new power becomes important in regard to the national curriculum. Headteachers can offer their governing bodies the option of a longer school day as a means of fitting the national curriculum into an overcrowded timetable. Many schools may feel the need for longer hours, so that pupils coming up for external examinations can cope with an increased load of coursework.

A change in the length of a school's working day would not affect the number of hours covered by the teachers' contract (1265). It would simply pre-empt more of the teachers' time to cover the timetable, leaving less for other prescribed activities.

Political balance
Section 45 of the 1986 Act gave governors, local authorities and headteachers the duty to secure 'a balanced presentation of opposing views' on controversial political topics in lessons or in school-organised extra-curricular activities. This, too, was a late addition to the Bill and added new responsibilities of an ill-defined nature to those already undertaken by governors.

Complaints
The governors are also a focal point for complaints and criticisms from parents and the community. The national curriculum is an entitlement: parents who believe it is not being provided, or is

being provided in an inadequate manner, have a channel of complaint leading to local appeals committees set up by the local authorities (Education Reform Act, Section 23). Appeals will only reach these bodies if governors have failed to satisfy the complainants on the way.

The governors' general responsibility for the conduct of the school means that their duties in regard to the national curriculum cannot be confined to a once-for-all curriculum review: it is up to the governors to take a *continuing* interest in the content of instruction. The co-opted members are expected to bring their background knowledge and concerns to these discussions – in particular, the concerns of business and employment – and, given the fact that the national curriculum is not intended to occupy the whole of the time available to the school, governors will expect to be informed about, and comment on, the range of options outside the prescribed minimum course of instruction, and the cross-curricular themes which extend the experience of pupils.

Discipline

The 1986 Act makes it clear that it is the headteacher who bears the main responsibility for making the school rules and enforcing them (Section 22(a)). The governors are expected to prepare 'a written statement of general principles'. The head's duty is to act 'in accordance with' this written statement, and to 'have regard to any guidance the governors may offer on particular matters'.

Here again, the governors have to exercise their general responsibility for the conduct of the school and its ethos, which includes the disciplinary character of the regime over which the head presides. The main working responsibility rests with the head and the staff.

The ultimate sanction at the disposal of the head is to suspend or expel a pupil for a breach of discipline. The law knows this as 'exclusion', temporary, indefinite or permanent. Detailed provisions in Sections 23 to 27 of the 1986 Education (No. 2) Act set out rules which have to be followed by heads, governing bodies and local authorities when an exclusion occurs. These are further covered in the Articles of Government, and local authorities also issue their own guidance on the matter. The rules are complicated and differ as between county, voluntary Controlled and maintained special schools on the one hand, and Aided and Special Agreement schools on the other.

The DES Circular (7/87) which provides a gloss on these sections of the 1986 Act makes it clear that the main object of the provisions for consultation between the local authority, the governors and the head, which must follow when a pupil is excluded, is to 'prevent exclusions from going on too long or indefinitely'. The Secretary of State 'assumes' that the great majority of exclusions will be brief: longer periods would require 'closer consideration'.

Governing bodies have to make up their own minds on the merits of each case. The Circular envisages exclusions of a few days as being endorsed or ended by 'Chairman's action'. If necessary, governors can consult quickly by telephone. Exceptionally, exclusion may be for a longer, possibly indefinite, term – as, for example, when specialist advice or diagnosis is being sought. If the headteacher or the governing body (whose decision is always binding on the head) do not come forward with a proposal for reinstatement, the local authority must force a decision by fixing a date. Then it is up to the head either to accept the local authority ruling or to make the exclusion permanent, in which case the local authority and the governors have to consider the situation afresh.

If a pupil is excluded permanently – expelled – there is a formal appeals procedure (under Section 26 of the 1986 Act): the parent (or the pupil, if over 18) can appeal against the exclusion or the governors could appeal against a reinstatement order. In maintained schools (other than Aided and Special Agreement) the decision of the appeal committee is binding. In the case of an Aided or Special Agreement school, the governors retain the right to decide whether to readmit an expelled student.

At every stage parents can make representations, and local arrangements may provide for rights of appeal in case of temporary or indefinite exclusion. The local authority retains a reserve power (Section 28) to step in with directions to the governors or head, in circumstances where it believes discipline has broken down or the school has become unmanageable – that is, if the behaviour of pupils or parents is such that the education of those

attending the school is, or is likely to become, 'severely prejudiced'. This does not apply to Aided or Special Agreement
schools, however, which are only obliged to 'consider any representation made to them by the authority'.

The rules are meant to be water-tight, but if the teachers'
unions take a hand, as at the Poundswick school in Manchester
in 1985–86, where a year-long dispute followed the exclusion of
five pupils, the situation can become much more complicated. If
union members feel their own professional authority is not being
upheld and refuse to accept a local authority instruction to
readmit an excluded pupil, what began as a matter of pupil
discipline turns into an industrial dispute. Normally a pupil
expelled from one school is admitted to another and given a fresh
chance, but if the teachers' morale is low or they have other
grievances, the circumstances may make this hard to achieve.
This can only add to the difficulty of dealing with cases of this
kind.

Appointments and dismissals of staff

The Education Reform Act 1988 extended the governors'
powers over appointments and dismissals. These powers are set
out in the section of the Act dealing with financial delegation,
which transfers to the governors powers formerly residing in the
local authority.

The powers over appointments are wide and extend to both
teaching and non-teaching staff. In the case of the most senior
staff – heads and deputies – governors have to consider the
advice which the LEA chief education officer must give. In other
appointments, the chief education officer must offer advice if
invited to do so. The head, too, has the right to advise on staff
appointments below the rank of head.

The governors of schools with financial delegation are responsible for firing as well as hiring (Education Reform Act 1988,
Section 36). Their powers as drafted seem draconian: in practice
they are curbed by agreements and by the costs incurred by
unfair or unreasonable behaviour. The local authority remains
the employer of the staff. The Act envisages that governors,
exercising their increased powers may want to dismiss certain
staff members or encourage them to take premature retirement.

In such circumstances, the cost of the dismissal or early retirement falls on the local authority unless the authority has 'good reason for deducting these costs' from the school's share of the education monies.

In Aided schools, the *governors* are the employers of the teachers and other staff, but the Act provides for the chief education officer to have a similar advisory role in senior appointments and for the costs of dismissals or early retirement to be covered by a similar rule.

Financial control

In schools which qualify for financial delegation, the governors have responsibility for spending and accounting for their share of the local authority's education spending. They have to exercise their powers in this respect in accordance with the authority's approved scheme. The Education Reform Act (Section 36(5)) underlines their wide discretion in spending the sums entrusted to them, and the fact that they can delegate their powers of financial management to the headteacher to the extent that the scheme allows.

Governors 'do not incur any personal liability in respect of anything done in good faith in the exercise or purported exercise' of their budgetary powers (Section 36(6)). As in all their activities in their capacity of governors, however, they lose their immunity if they are negligent. In principle, they must take as much care in attending to governing body business as they would in looking after their own affairs. This liability can be covered by insurance; local practice varies.

Local school management is going to change the nature of governors' responsibilities, both in county and voluntary schools, and will certainly increase the need to recruit more governors with expertise in management and finance.

In so far as financial delegation under Part 1, Chapter 3 of the Education Reform Act increases the resources over which governors exercise a discretion, it should (in theory) be possible for governing bodies to reflect their own educational priorities in resource allocation at the school level. What local authorities, governors and headteachers will have to do is to reconcile the sometimes divergent provisions of the 1944 Education Act and the 1986 and 1988 Acts. Governors have a statutory right to modify the local authority's curriculum policy in drawing up their own. Local authorities have to respect this right in the conditions they attach to the budgets they distribute. A determined local authority is certainly allowed to earmark funds to be spent on its own priority projects (if the Secretary of State approves its scheme), and to keep those earmarked funds separate from those distributed by formula as schools' budget shares. The DES will clearly be looking to curb local authority schemes which (in the words of the Circular) 'cut across the discretion and duties that governors are given' in the new legal framework.

The Circular also shows the Secretary of State's thinking on the clause in Section 37 which empowers a local authority to withdraw a governing body's delegated powers, when governors are guilty of 'substantial or persistent failure' to comply with the scheme; or where the funds in their care are not being managed 'in a satisfactory manner'.

Withdrawal of powers is clearly seen as a last resort, and not to be used till other methods of persuasion and enforcement have been exhausted. It would be for the local authority to determine in each case whether a school's failure to deliver the national curriculum (and 'the local authority's curriculum policy as modified by the governing body') would justify the withdrawal of delegated powers.

There is room for argument about the extent of the governors' powers to 'modify' the local authority's curriculum policy. Clearly, the Secretary of State would want governing bodies to have the right to ignore the more extreme demands of an education authority which is seeking to advance its own political ideology through a curriculum policy. But, as has been pointed out, 'modify' does not mean the same as 'reject out of hand' and time will tell how the term is interpreted, case by disputed case.

Similarly, 'substantial or persistent' can only be interpreted within the context of a particular school's activities. If the governors appealed against the local authority's decision to withdraw delegated powers, the Secretary of State would then have to make his own ruling.

Charges

Another new duty imposed on governors relates to the sections of the Education Reform Act on charges levied on parents for activities connected with the schools (Sections 106–111). These sections forbid charging for admission to school and for all in-school curricular tuition, except in regard to instrumental music. Within the terms of the legislation, there is a range of activities and optional extras for which charges may be made.

Local authorities have to formulate their own policies on charging in connection with their schemes of financial delegation. And governors, too, will have discretion (within their delegated budgets) to decide what charges to make. They will not, of course, be expected to levy charges for activities, the full cost of which is covered by the local authority under its scheme of delegation.

Section 110 makes it a statutory duty for the governing body of a maintained school (and every local education authority) to formulate and keep under review a policy on charges.

Reports and meetings

Governors must send a written report to parents once a year on the work of the school (and the governors), and hold an annual parents' meeting where this report can be presented and discussed (Sections 30 and 31, Education (No. 2) Act 1986). The report must list all the governors, and state their method of appointment (e.g. elected parent, co-opted, local authority representative). It must contain a financial statement showing how the budget has been spent. It must summarise the examination and assessment results and describe the steps taken to strengthen links with the community (including the police).

Every parent should have a copy of the report not less than two weeks before the annual parents' meeting. The governors have the responsibility of deciding exactly who should be regarded as a parent for the purpose of the annual meeting (as also for parent-governor elections and ballots on opting out).

Grant-maintained status

Under the 1988 Act, the governors of local authority maintained schools have the power to initiate a change to grant-maintained status (see Chapter 4). Grant-maintained school governors' powers will be determined by the Articles of Government approved for each school by the Secretary of State. The majority of the governors will be those in the 'first' or 'foundation' categories nominated by the promoters of the change of status. Their responsibilities will be akin to those of Aided school governors. Their allocated resources will be similar to those of local authority maintained schools but with fewer deductions for services provided by the authority.

Further education
The same principles which have been applied to school governors in the 1986 and 1988 Acts are extended by the 1988 Act to local authority colleges of further education, along with delegated financial control within local authority strategic plans.

The composition of F.E. governing bodies is set out in Section 152 (see Chapter 6): the strong representation of industry and commerce is intended to reduce the local authority's influence and increase the colleges' responsiveness to local business needs.

Conclusion
The recent spate of educational legislation has altered the role of governors and increased their responsibilities. Governors, therefore, need to be aware of the Articles of Government under which they operate, and the guidance offered by their local authorities. There are also training courses offered by local authorities, university departments, voluntary organisations like the National Association of Governors and Managers, and the Open University. *The Law of Education*, edited by Peter Liell and John B. Saunders (Butterworths), provides an invaluable commentary on the law as it affects governors among the army of professionals and lay persons who operate the education service.

It would be a mistake to suggest, however, that school governors need to become armchair lawyers. The legal changes are less important than the change in attitudes which the 1986 and 1988 Acts have brought about. What is *expected* of school governors has changed. This applies to the governors of Aided schools as well as those of county and Controlled schools. The presence of a much larger number of parent-governors means that governing bodies will be kept in much more direct touch with the concerns of the users.

Parent-governors will be among those to whom parents first turn with a problem or a grievance. They will be expected to take up such problems and seek answers from heads. If they do not get satisfaction they will expect to bring these matters to a meeting of the governing body. Whether they like it or not, governors are going to be drawn into the discussion of the internal regime of the school – the school's private life – and this, in turn, will mean that governors spend more time at the school and expect to be shown more of what is going on.

Similarly, co-opted members will be expected to represent outside interests – in industry, commerce or the community at large – and seek to use their position as governors to make the school pay more attention to their causes. All this adds up, once again, to the governors' responsibility for the ethos of the school – for the 'hidden' curriculum as well as the public one. They have a licence to interfere (a busy-bodies' charter?); the new consumerism commits them to a new approach.

Cynics will assume that a competent headteacher will quickly learn how to thwart these interventionist tendencies. This will undoubtedly be what happens in many places, much of the time: it will be an important part of the head's management task to 'manage' the governors – to prevent the laymen and laywomen from pushing the school off course by their enthusiasms or their prejudices, and to divert their interfering tendencies along lines of the head's own choosing, persuading them that his or her own pet schemes were first thought of by them.

Many governing bodies will willingly play their part in the beneficial charades in which heads will manoeuvre them. But only up to a point. It is no part of the governors' job to surrender their critical faculties. Up and down the country there is a small but significant number of schools which are failing because the headteacher's leadership is inadequate and the governors have either failed to recognise the fact or to discover how to pull the levers to do something about it.

Doing something about it is unlikely to be primarily a legal matter. It is likely to have a lot more to do with close liaison with the local authority and its advisers, to assemble the evidence of what is wrong and thereby to persuade the head that early retirement is the best option. The 1988 Act strengthens the governors' hand, but action still depends on getting the professional advice and inspection reports with which to back up a determination to bring about a change at the top.

It is only right that it should be very difficult to sack a headteacher. Heads are open to unsubstantiated accusations and to criticisms which are not backed up with facts. It would be thoroughly unsatisfactory if a body of lay governors could easily send the head packing just for being unpopular or because they fail to get on with him or her. Notwithstanding the governors' increased powers of hire and fire, they will still have to work hard and show great determination if they decide to call the head's position into question.

The 1988 Act has introduced an important new factor in the form of the testing and assessment procedures set up in connection with the national curriculum. These will produce a steady flow of information about performance which, from one year to the next, will produce some evidence of progress or retreat.

The position will change with financial delegation, too, because the local authority will be expected to monitor the performance of the schools and hold them accountable for the use of delegated funds. Governors will themselves be under scrutiny, along with the schools for which they are responsible. In-service training and admonition will be the main weapons in the hands of the monitoring authorities. If the DES is successful in refining a wide range of performance indicators, these too will be used to hold the schools, and all who share in them, accountable.

Notes
1. Scottish Education Department consultative papers on School Boards, August 1987 and January 1988.
2. Stuart Maclure, *A History of Education in London*, 1870–1990, Allen Lane, 1990.

3. The Taylor Report, *A New Partnership for our Schools*, HMSO, 1977.
4. *Parental Influence at School*, A DES Green Paper, Cmnd 9242, HMSO, 1984.
5. DES, *Circular 7/87: Education (No. 2) Act, 1986, Further Guidance*.

10

Perspective: From 1944 to 1988

To understand the full impact of the Education Reform Act of 1988 it is necessary to consider its relationship to the Education Act of 1944, and some of the ways in which dominant ideas about education, society and the economy changed in the four decades which separate the two major pieces of legislation.

On the face of it, the authors of the 1988 Act overturned the received wisdom which had held sway in the public and professional discussion of education in post-war England. Of course the received wisdom was never universally acknowledged. To talk of 'dominant ideas' implies that at any time there were those who dissented. But no one could deny that the education sections of the Conservative manifesto at the 1987 General Election and the Bill which followed put 'the liberal educational establishment' on the defensive. The progressives found themselves cast as conservatives defending the status quo – a status quo which incorporated the failures, as well as the triumphs, of the system which had grown up under the banner of the 1944 Act.

How this transformation came about goes far beyond the record of educational development and pedagogy. It turned on larger social and political questions which related the aims of education to those of society. How those questions were answered, created the opportunity seized by the radical Conservatives in 1988, within a framework of political ideology which substituted an individualistic, 'enterprise' culture for the once-fashionable collective virtues and imperfections of the Welfare State.

What is clear on examination is that the received wisdom and the established verities had been undermined over a period of time, not suddenly in 1987. What seemed to many people like a *bouleversement* for which they were unprepared was the culmination of a longer process of change which had taken place piecemeal and unevenly, as public perceptions of the socio-political purposes of education and the administrative and professional means of delivering an education service, altered.

Climates of opinion

Nobody can read very far into the post-war period without sensing the idealism and the optimism – some of it pretty daft, but none the less genuine – which pervaded the discussion of educational reform. The same was true of the Welfare State as a whole, but it was especially so in regard to education, which was much less politically contentious than – say – the creation of a National Health Service.

Many of the sentiments were naive in the extreme – not least the benign assumption that people were generally agreed about the aims of education, vocational, cultural, personal – and the belief in some Adam Smith-like divine hand which would miraculously ensure that the sum of all these individual aims would add up to the essential aims of society – the basic premise on which a publicly-provided child-centred education depended.

There was an assumption that education (at almost any level) was a good thing in itself – a self-justifying benefit to the commonwealth. This was the strongest and longest-lasting element in this liberal public philosophy. It lasted till the mid-1970s. It certainly lasted till Mrs Thatcher's White Paper on *A Framework for Expansion*[1] in 1972, which was the last major educational document in which this assumption is implicit. The belief that education is a self-justifying good was an article of faith not a tentative hypothesis. Perhaps it is the loss of this faith which separates the educational discourse of the 1980s most sharply from that of the earlier period. The rhetoric has changed – moved away from a concern with 'the whole person' and 'education for life' to a much more sceptical insistence that education must be useful in some directly marketable way – producing employable skills or nationally-needed expertise or character attributes required by industry or commerce.

Nowhere was the post-war optimism more clearly illustrated

than in the pamphlets published by the Ministry of Education in the late 1940s. Take, for example, the much-quoted Pamphlet Number 9, *The New Secondary Education*,[2] now a favourite butt for hind-sighted comprehensive school campaigners, eager to put Ellen Wilkinson, Labour's first post-war Education Minister, in a dock of their own making. This painted a glowing picture of the liberation which was offered to those hitherto held in thrall to the elementary school code:

> 'It is important [she wrote in the Foreword] not to make plans that are too rigid. . . . The schools must have freedom to experiment, room to grow, variety for the sake of freshness, for the fun of it even. Laughter in the classroom, self-confidence growing every day, eager interest instead of bored conformity.'

The examples could be multiplied, and they provide an authentic flavour of the time as well as a guide to the movement of opinion inside the Ministry of Education and, in particular, inside the Inspectorate.

The depth to which these liberal sentiments penetrated is, of course, a matter for sceptical speculation. But what the official rhetoric shows is that the spirit of Plowden was already firmly established in the early post-war days, even though the practice of the kind of progressive methods which Plowden endorsed was, as Neville Bennett and others[3] have shown, never, even at the apogee of this particular movement, as widespread as its proponents hoped or its enemies feared.

The contrast between then and now can be clearly seen if you compare the language and sentiments of those early post-war pamphlets with the flood of material now emanating from the Inspectorate and the Department of Education and Science. The 1980s material is also humane and the tone is still, for the most part, unauthoritarian. But the public values, the emphasis, the tone of voice and the unspoken assumptions have changed, in line with the spirit of the times.

Milestones
It is not difficult to see some of the milestones which mark changes in the climate of opinion since the 1950s. Some of them

are associated with the rise and fall of the curriculum development movement in the 1960s and 1970s – the life cycle of the
Schools Council (1964–1983) and the tension generated by the
notion of a teacher-controlled curriculum built into the constitution of that body. Somewhere along the line the progressives got
too far ahead of the game and opened the door for a strenuous
popular reaction. None of this can be divorced from the rise and
fall of sociology as queen of the social sciences and the main-
spring of educational research and policy analysis.

Student unrest at the end of the 1960s sent shock waves
through all the developed countries, which reinforced the tendency towards reaction. In the nature of things it is difficult to
calculate the long-term effect of *les événements de '68* in Paris, or
the free speech confrontation at Berkeley, or the scenes at the
London School of Economics or the University of Essex, on the
development of public opinion over a generation. But that these
episodes left a lasting impression on the public mind few can
doubt. They helped to destroy some of the illusions about the
benefits which more education might bring; they confirmed the
doubts of those who had never gone along with the progressive
ideology. The participants in the 'student rebellions' were the
first fruit of the post-war world – the baby-boom generation.
They, too, emerged from the excitement, disillusioned.

One of those seared by the troubles in higher education was
Mrs Caroline Cox – later Baroness Cox and an energetic right-
wing skirmisher in the House of Lords debates on the Education
Reform Bill – who experienced at first hand the strife which tore
the North London Polytechnic apart in the 1970s. Her account of
the events at the college, which appeared as *Rape of Reason*
(1975), launched her political career and gave her an entry into
the group of new Right intellectuals who began to interest
themselves in education. With Dr John Marks she published a
succession of books and pamphlets attacking such targets as the
Inner London Education Authority, and the activities of politically motivated local authorities and teachers. In particular, she
sought to compare the standards of achievement of the comprehensive schools with those of the remaining grammar schools
and secondary modern schools. This took Cox and Marks into a
treacherous field of statistical analysis, attempting to discount

(or not discount) school performance for extraneous social factors. The work was much criticised by academics specialising in such matters, but there was a robustness about their work, and polemic quality, which put the 'experts' on the defensive. The new Right depended more on the energy and robustness of such contributions than on the depth of analysis or the penetration of the ideas. A battle of ideologies was in progress, not a cool and rational debate.

The first Black Paper appeared in 1969.[4] For all its manifest limitations as an analysis of what was right and wrong with the schools, it struck a nerve. It made an impact which showed that there were a great many people outside the charmed circle of the education system who were waiting to challenge the cosy view of educational progress which had become the received wisdom. Public opinion was waiting for a lead – for reaction to be made respectable. Those who suspected that the progressive Emperor had no clothes but were afraid to say so, took courage. Populist politicians took up the hue and cry. Dr Rhodes Boyson – now Sir Rhodes Boyson MP – then still a London headteacher, immediately began to put together a political pressure group to follow up the Black Paper initiative, and what became the Council for Educational Standards was formed. This was the first of a series of similar right-wing educational pressure groups – often the same people wearing different hats – which came to include such bodies as the Campaign for Real Education, the National Grammar School Association, Parental Alliance for Choice in Education, and Parents for English Education Rights.[5]

The proliferation of such bodies followed, with the Centre for Policy Studies, the think-tank formed in 1974 by Sir Keith Joseph and Mrs Margaret Thatcher, providing a focus for new Right thinking and the confident expression of hitherto unfashionable views. Part of the story is about bringing views which were once regarded as unacceptable into common currency. In this way, the Right changed the boundaries of debate.

Any discussion of these events inevitably focuses on the Ruskin College speech in 1976 by the then Prime Minister, James Callaghan. This formally marked the bi-partisan acknowledgement that the post-war educational hypotheses were to be replaced by a different, less generous, perhaps more realistic, certainly more utilitarian set of views. It was significant that it fell to a Labour prime minister to hoist the signal – bringing out the main headings under which the reappraisal of the education system would be conducted in the Great Debate, so-called, which he launched.

A text of the speech appeared in *The Times Educational Supplement* on 22 October 1976. Mr Callaghan said:

> . . . "There is nothing wrong with non-educationalists, even a Prime Minister, talking about. . . . [education]. . . . Everyone is allowed to put his oar in on how to overcome our economic problems, how to put the balance of payments right, how to secure more exports and so on and so on. Very important too. But, I venture to say, not as important in the long run as preparing future generations for life . . . .
>
> 'I take it that no one claims exclusive rights in this field. Public interest is strong and will be satisfied. It is legitimate. We spend £6 billion a year on education, so there will be discussion. But let it be rational. If everything is reduced to such phrases as "educational freedom versus state control" we shall get nowhere. I repeat that parents, teachers, learned and professional bodies, representatives of higher education and both sides of industry, together with the Government, all have an important part to play in formulating and expressing the purpose of education and the standards that we need.
>
> 'During my travels around the country in recent months, I have had many discussions that show concern about some of these matters.
>
> 'First let me say, so that there should be no misunderstanding, that I have been very impressed by a number of the schools I have visited, by the enthusiasm and dedication of the teaching profession, by the variety of courses that are offered in our comprehensive schools, especially in arts and crafts as well as in other subjects, and by the alertness and keenness of many of the young people I have met . . . .
>
> 'But I am concerned on my journeys to find complaints from industry that new recruits from the schools sometimes do not have the basic tools to do the job that is required.

'I have been concerned to find that many of our best trained students who have completed the higher levels of education at university or polytechnic have no desire or intention of joining industry. Their preferences are to stay in academic life (very pleasant, I know) or to find their way into the civil service. There seems to be a need for a more technological bias in science teaching that will lead towards practical applications in industry rather than towards academic studies.

'Or, to take other examples, why is it, as I am told, that such a high proportion of girls abandon science before they leave school? Then there is concern about the standards of numeracy of school leavers. Is there not a case for a professional review of the mathematics needed by industry at different levels? To what extent are these deficiencies the result of insufficient coordination between schools and industry? Indeed how much of the criticism about the absence of basic skills and attitudes is due to industry's own shortcomings rather than to the educational system? Why is it that 30,000 vacancies for students in science and engineering in our universities and polytechnics were not taken up last year while the humanities courses were full?

'On another aspect there is the unease felt by parents and teachers about the new informal methods of teaching which seem to produce excellent results when they are in well-qualified hands but are much more dubious in their effects when they are not. They seem to be best accepted, if I may judge from my own experience, where there are strong parent/teacher links. There is little wrong with the range and diversity of our courses. But is there sufficient thoroughness and depth in those required in after life to make a living?

'These are proper subjects for discussion and debate. And it should be a rational debate based on the facts. My remarks are not a clarion call to Black Paper prejudices. We all know those who claim to defend standards but who in reality are simply seeking to defend old privileges and inequalities.

'It is not my intention to become enmeshed in such

problems as whether there should be a basic curriculum with universal standards – although I am inclined to think that there should be – nor about other issues on which there is a divided professional opinion such as the position and role of the Inspectorate. . . . What I am saying is that where there is legitimate public concern it will be to the advantage of all involved in the education field if these concerns are aired and shortcomings righted or fears are put to rest.

'To the critics I would say that we must carry the teaching profession with us. They have the expertise and they have the professional approach. To the teachers I would say that you must satisfy the parents and industry that what you are doing meets their requirements and the needs of their children. For if the public is not convinced then the profession will be laying up trouble for itself in the future.

'The goals of our education, from nursery school through to adult education, are clear enough. They are to equip children to the best of their ability for a lively, constructive place in society and also to fit them to do a job of work. Not one or the other, but both.

'For many years – as I remember perhaps better than most because I am older – the accent was simply on fitting a so-called inferior group of children, and many of you would have been in that category, with just enough learning to earn their living in the factory. Labour has attacked that attitude consistently, during 60 or 70 years and throughout my childhood. There is now widespread recognition of the need to cater for a child's personality, to let it flower in the fullest possible way.

'The balance was wrong in the past. We have a responsibility now in this generation to see that we do not get it wrong in the other direction. There is no virtue in producing socially well adjusted members of society who are unemployed because they do not have the skills. Nor at the other extreme must they be technically efficient robots. Both of the basic purposes of education require the same essential tools. These are to be basically literate, to be basically numerate, to understand how to live and work together, to have respect for others and respect for the individual. . . .

'There has been a massive injection of resources into education, mainly to meet increased numbers, partly to raise standards. But in present circumstances there is little expectation of further increased resources being made available, at any rate for the time being. I fear that those whose only answer to these problems is to call for more money are going to be disappointed. But that surely cannot be the end of the matter. There is a challenge to us all in these days and the challenge in education is to examine its priorities and to secure as high efficiency as you can by the skilful use of the £6 billion of existing resources.

'Let me repeat some of the fields that need study because they cause concern. There are the methods and aims of informal instruction. The strong case for the so-called core curriculum of basic knowledge. What is the proper way of monitoring the use of resources in order to maintain a proper national standard of performance? What is the role of the inspectorate in relation to national standards and their maintenance? And there is the need to improve relations between industry and education.'

The speech served notice on the educators, in very gentle terms, that the Government had serious doubts about what the schools were doing, and intended to clear up these doubts even if this meant invading areas which the teachers thought were their territory.

It set up the bogus antithesis between education for life and education for a job, and in knocking down the Aunt Sally, implied that the education system had failed to give due weight to the vocational aspect. An agenda already existed in the so-called Yellow Book, the brief which the DES had produced for the Prime Minister's office in advance of the speech.[6]

One set of items in the Ruskin speech concerned *education as preparation for work*. Mr Callaghan endorsed employers' criticisms of poor standards, and noted the preference for arts and pure science over technology and for jobs in government and academe rather than industry.

Another set of criticisms applied to *teaching methods and the curriculum*, with a scarcely veiled attack on progressive primary methods and a call for a core curriculum. A third set related to *teachers and their professionalism*, their willingness to share curriculum concerns with the parents and the public, their accountability. Among the remedies he put forward for discussion was a more interventionalist role for the Inspectorate and the DES, more lay influence in and through governing bodies, and a new deal for the 16–19s (a foreshadowing of future youth training initiatives).

Between 1976 and 1985 – between the Ruskin speech and *Better Schools*, Sir Keith Joseph's White Paper issued in March 1985[7] – the DES worked through this agenda. A now forgotten Green Paper issued in 1977 – *Education in Schools* – laid out a programme affecting the curriculum, the management of the teaching force, the training of teachers, standards and assessment, and school and working life.[8] It summed up the administrators' approach to the restructuring of the education system to bring it, by incremental stages, from the 1960s into the 1980s.

This incrementalist approach survived well into the era initiated by Mrs Thatcher's election victory in 1979. A raft of measures, leading up to the incorporation of the national curriculum in the 1988 Education Act, can be traced directly to the policies elaborated in the Department of Education and Science in the years after the Ruskin speech.

Keen observers such as Ted Tapper and Brian Salter, the University of Sussex political scientists who have written extensively about the evolution of educational policy in this period,[9] have noted the emergence of a strong Department view at the DES. There is no doubt that the Department responded to the opportunity which arose in the mid-1970s to take an active role, in areas where hitherto the DES had been obliged to tread carefully. Sir William Pile, the Permanent Secretary from 1970 to 1976 had already begun to prepare the ground by strengthening the Inspectorate and opening the way for it to reassert its inspectorial role over that of friendly advice. In 1974, he had 'wondered aloud' to a visiting team from OECD 'whether the Government could continue to debar itself from what had been termed "the secret garden" of the curriculum'. A year later, in evidence to the House of Commons Select Committee, he had gone out of his way to invite MPs to press for DES intervention in the curriculum,[10] and when eventually the call came from Downing Street to draw up the Yellow Book (by which time Sir William had left to become chairman of the Inland Revenue Board) the Department was ready to exploit the opening.

The DES has been sniped at by such critics as Lord Donoughue (who as Mr Bernard Donoughue headed Mr Callaghan's policy unit at No. 10) for being slow to respond and imprisoned in the conventions of decentralised administration.[11] Tapper and Salter reached opposite conclusions and detected a 'bureaucratic dynamic located in the central apparatus, the Department of Education and Science'. In their view, the DES was an 'ambitious bureaucracy' which maintained a managerial continuity which was not interrupted by ministerial changes and general elections.

Some critics have seen this strong Departmental view as in some way reprehensible. In reality it is one of the essential functions of the DES to provide continuity and steadiness. The policies which officials put forward in 1976 formed a package which ministers adopted, and they were sustained over time by successive secretaries of state who had nothing better to put in their place.

The tone and tenor of post-1976 educational policy was markedly different from that of the post-war period. It incorporated a measured reaction against the progressive era. It reflected a changed world: the world of the 1970s when Britain went through a deeply depressing period of economic decline, with unemployment – the dragon which the post-war celebrants of the Welfare State believed they had slain – rising to levels unseen since 1939.

The 1970s was the decade of rocketing oil prices and galloping inflation; of industrial unrest and the attempt to placate organised labour by 'social contracts' which invited the unions to concede wage restraint in return for political power. It was the decade of pessimism about Britain's ability or will to compete in international trade – the decade when the International Monetary Fund took over the management of the economy and imposed strict monetary discipline on a government to whose traditional supporters such policies were anathema.

These were the years in which the retreat from the Welfare

State came to be acknowledged, tacitly, on the Left as well as on the Right. For the traditional progressive, this was deeply depressing. It did not necessarily lead to an active rejection of the institutions of the Welfare State – rather a fatalistic acceptance that former hopes were not being realised in the National Health Service and the social services without any active desire to see the apparatus of welfare dismantled.

But taken all in all, it added up to the climatic change in public opinion which by the end of the 1970s saw the Left in desperate disarray, with the Labour Government battening down the hatches, at loggerheads with the trade unions and preparing for a landslide electoral defeat.

When Sir Keith Joseph went to the DES as Secretary of State in 1981 he was determined to apply in education the logic of the Government's radical economic policies. He distrusted the incremental approach. Even more, he distrusted the attempt to build such an approach on the basis of consensus among the education providers. He wanted to go for structural reforms which would increase parental choice and make the education system respond to the healthy discipline of competition and market forces.

The idea of education vouchers has come up from time to time in earlier chapters – it could be said to have hovered in the background as the Education Reform Act (which nowhere mentions vouchers) went through. A voucher scheme was the device which Sir Keith and his intellectual allies believed capable of revolutionising relationships in education and providing a short-cut to the higher standards which must come (in theory at least) from giving more power to parent-consumers.

But Sir Keith Joseph's attempt to make quick progress on vouchers failed. Though he made it his first priority, and in his early months at the Department showed serious interest in little else, he was unable to devise a voucher scheme which looked feasible within the sort of time-span which was politically realistic. Nor could he get agreement on a pilot scheme which might have paved the way for a more general plan.

By the General Election of 1983 his civil servants had succeeded in convincing him that the practical difficulties in the way of a voucher system were unsuperable in the timescale within which he had to work. In particular, he was confronted with major difficulties of an expensive transition which neither he, nor the Prime Minister, was prepared to face. He dropped the idea of vouchers before the 1983 General Election. Mrs Thatcher endorsed this decision.

Sir Keith then began, somewhat belatedly, to devote his full attention to the more modest reforms which were already in the pipeline – the new GCSE, the overhaul of teacher training, a new teachers' contract and the attempt to introduce an appraisal scheme for teachers. He also cooperated closely with the Manpower Services Commission in the Technical and Vocational Education Initiative, and used his office and his rhetoric to advance the cause of 'the bottom 40 per cent' whom he believed to be neglected in most comprehensive schools.

The Joseph prescription was, essentially, the Callaghan consensus in action. This was frequently obscured by Sir Keith's own unpopularity at the height of the long-drawn industrial dispute about teachers' pay and conditions; his political clumsiness helped to prolong the dispute and hold back progress on many of the projects closest to his heart. What he contributed to the radical reforms which followed his departure from office, however, was of central importance: a heightened public anxiety.

He had felt it his duty to dwell on the education system's shortcomings, the ineffective teachers whom nobody sacked, the 'bottom 40 per cent' who were short-changed, the low expectations which were all too often fulfilled. By so doing he angered the teachers, irritated the local authorities, but helped to prepare public opinion for radical change. In this he found himself in an unholy alliance with the teachers who, by their injudicious industrial action, were antagonising the same public opinion and convincing many who were not directly involved that, sooner or later, someone would have to take the educational system in hand.

It had been a necessary part of the case put together by radical critics on the Right that 'standards had fallen' as a result of the ideology of the progressives and their egalitarian suspicion of both elitism and excellence. Evidence to support this thesis had, however, been hard to present in an intellectually convincing form. The examination statistics showed that the number of students achieving examination success had continued to rise as a proportion of the relevant age groups, though more slowly in the 1970s and 1980s than in the earlier period. This did not support the cry of 'falling standards'. But there was a suspicion, not confined to the extreme Right, that this was a mechanical contrivance: the mechanics of the examination system ensured that if more candidates presented themselves more would succeed, and that there would be subtle adjustment of standards to make this happen.

The evidence which the new Right had hoped for, but had not found, came in 1983 when Professor Sig Prais of the National Institute of Economic and Social Research published a paper on mathematics standards comparing levels of performance in England and in the Federal Republic of Germany.[12] Using surveys prepared for the International Educational Achievement Study (1964) and supplementing these with a detailed examination of syllabuses and examinations in the two countries, Professor Prais concluded that German pupils in the *bottom half of the ability range* (attending schools corresponding roughly to secondary modern schools) achieved average levels of performance comparable with the average for the *whole range of ability* in England and Wales. If this were so, the performance for the 'bottom 40 per cent' in England could, therefore, be confidently declared to be well below that of the same group of pupils in one of Britain's main European competitor nations.

The importance of the Prais findings was that they moved the argument away from sterile wrangling about how standards now compared with standards at some hypothetical time in the past. The Prais evidence suggested that, whatever was the truth about the past, the present performance of English boys and girls compared badly with that of German boys and girls. As Germany was one of Britain's main international competitors the importance of the findings was plain. Technical arguments about cross-cultural differences faded in the face of elementary facts about the contrast between the mathematics available to (and demanded from) apprentice electricians, say, in England and Germany.

Professor Prais also put forward explanations of the difference. He attributed the superior performance of German schools to their clearly defined, more sharply focused, programmes of study and fewer teacher-led variations from school to school and area to area.

The Prais contribution had the special significance of telling would-be reformers what they wanted to hear. It helped reinforce the idea of an education system in crisis and gave further rational support for the idea of a national curriculum, tightly controlled to avoid variations in professional practice and monitored by regular testing.

Market forces

Sir Keith Joseph's retreat on vouchers was a great disappointment to the radical Right. The long-serving exponents of the application of market forces to educational decision-making were the economists and political scientists associated with the Institute of Economic Affairs (IEA). They believed that Sir Keith had had the wool pulled over his eyes by his senior officials in the DES, and were determined to keep the voucher issue alive.

The IEA was founded in 1955 to promote research and analysis on economic and social policy, with a strong basis in free-market economics. Early on, it became interested in the possibility of separating the financing of education from the provision of educational institutions. Taking up the voucher idea propounded in an article in 1955 by Professor Milton Friedman, the IEA published a provocative study by Dr E. G. West, *Education and the State* (1965).[13] This study examined the circumstances in which publicly-provided education was introduced in 1870, and gave an unusually enthusiastic account of the pre-existent market in schooling which the Forster Act effectively undermined. Subsequent books and pamphlets by such economists and political analysts as Mark Blaug, Stanley Dennison, Alan Maynard, Alan Peacock and the indefatigable Arthur Seldon, assembled a literature on vouchers in the English context to set alongside similar studies in the United States. Through these activities over many years, the IEA built up an effective network of academics and politicians interested in translating economic ideas into educational policy and policy into action.

The voucher idea was simple: to put the power of choice and decision-making in the hand of the consumer and take it away from the provider. This could be done by giving parents vouchers equivalent in value to the cost of their children's education in existing schools. They could then use these vouchers to 'buy' education from the school of their choice. Schools would cease to be 'maintained' by public authorities. Instead they would depend for funds on the fees they could charge, to be met, wholly or partly, from the vouchers.

There was room for any number of variants. The scheme could be limited to the present state sector or could extend to what is now the independent sector too. The voucher could be fixed at a flat rate – so much a head for all children. Or it could be weighted geographically, or to express social priorities. The voucher could be taxed or not taxed. . . .

The IEA approached the matter from the standpoint of free-market economics, not from any particular knowledge or experience of educational administration. The Institute took it for granted, on grounds of economic theory, that it must be more efficient to put the power of choice in the hands of the consumer, rather than the provider. The IEA's interest in education vouchers was matched by a devotion to health vouchers. It was underpinned by a series of sophisticated opinion polls, which ran from 1965 to 1987 and which have consistently shown that families would much prefer to exercise these choices themselves, and if necessary would use their own money to add to, or top up, the value of the voucher.

The voucher lobby reacted to the setback when Sir Keith Joseph backed down on vouchers in 1983 by redoubling their arguments and their attempts to persuade those with the ear of the politicians to try again. Sir Keith had passed on to the IEA a memorandum setting out the DES reasons for disputing the feasibility of going ahead. In 1983, the practical difficulties were compounded by political difficulties – a General Election was looming and the Conservatives did not have a workable scheme to put to the electorate. The IEA chewed over the DES memorandum, circulated it to its network of correspondents and did the groundwork for a renewed assault on the Secretary of State.

One of the outcomes of this was a paperback, *The Riddle of the Voucher* by Arthur Seldon,[14] which included suggestions for half-way houses and stepping-stones – changes in the way education was managed which fell short of the introduction of a voucher scheme, but which paved the way for such a move later on. Two of these have a direct bearing on the formulation of the policies which found their way into the Education Reform Act – not as being the prototype of specific changes, but as an indication of how the radical Right was thinking in 1985–86.

Professor Alan Peacock put forward proposals for a taxable voucher to help pay fees at private schools. Parents would have to apply for such a voucher, to 'contract in'. Initially, therefore it would be a scheme to benefit private education, but the value of the vouchers would be deducted from the central grants paid to the local county or borough where the voucher-holder lived. From such a modest beginning it would be possible to move towards a 'contracting out' scheme. The next stop would be for all parents to be credited with the taxable voucher unless they expressly applied to be excluded. Choice would thereby be enlarged. Once parents experienced choice they would come to insist on it.

The voucher people put great virtue on bringing the private school sector into the scheme. They had, therefore, to contend with the cost of providing vouchers for parents who had hitherto paid their own way, and the political cost of this subsidisation of privilege. By charging the cost of the voucher back to the local education authority where the claimant lived, the Peacock scheme met some of the financial arguments, but not the political ones. The voucher lobby believed the political objections were overstated: they had empirical evidence from their opinion polls that the public was not nearly as hostile to independent education as the politicians tended to imagine. They believed they could show that private schooling was popular, and that many more people were prepared to pay fees than the 6–7 per cent who now do so, if the fees were subsidised.

Another scheme, put forward and rejected about the time of

the 1983 General Election, bears a closer relationship to one of the cornerstones of the 1988 Reform Act.

The aim was to get people used to the idea of *per capita* funding. (The Education Reform Act does this by making local education authorities distribute money to their schools according to a formula based on the numbers and ages of the pupils.) The IEA proposal had been for the central government grant-in-aid for education to local authorities to be paid as a *per capita* payment for each pupil. This would have been a much less subtle and flexible method than the one built into Chapter Three of the 1988 Act. But what both schemes had in common is the establishment of something like a fee-structure. Once this was established, the voucher lobby believed it would be simple to go to the next stage and make the *per capita* payment to the parent instead of the school. The result would be a voucher – it could hardly be a cash payment – and its currency could be extended to the private sector as and when it was deemed to be expedient.

A new Act
By the year 1986, the Conservatives had already begun to think about the challenge of a third term of office and the need to maintain their radical momentum. A Cabinet Committee was busy considering proposals for education, and a steady succession of leaks to the lobby correspondents brought news of ideas said to be in the pipeline. These included suggestions that there might be new-style direct-grant schools, with or without a technological bias.

Sir Keith Joseph caused a sensation by telling an audience in Birmingham, as an afterthought, that he was interested in establishing some direct-grant primary schools.[15] The leaks and rumours covered every eventuality from city technology colleges to grant-maintained schools, along with many other ideas which fell by the wayside.

What eventually emerged in the election manifesto – and therefore ultimately in the Act – was assembled in secret in the nine months before the 1987 General Election. There was a determined effort *not* to consult the DES or the civil servants or chief education officers or local politicians. Under the discreet eye of Professor Brian Griffiths, head of the Prime Minister's